Jamestown Commitment

the Episcopal Church and the American Indian

by
Owanah Anderson

Forward Movement Publications, Cincinnati, Ohio

Jamestown Commitment is the first Indian-written book-length examination of the long history of Anglican/Episcopal mission among native peoples of the United States. It is a breakthrough in its assessment of the impact of the Gospel upon native lives across the continent. In spite of its breadth, the work never loses sight of the vital human element in the story of mission. The book is a compelling account from the very start down to the present day renewal of Indian mission.

C. B. Clark, American Indian Studies,
California State University, Long Beach
Secretary, NCIW

As I have travelled throughout the Episcopal Church, I have become personally aware of how much of our history has remained hidden from me. As I met with each community of faith in our domestic and overseas dioceses, the history and traditions of the faithful have been shared with me. The experiences of pain, of triumph, of dedication to proclamation of the Gospel and of sacrificial service were relived in each place, so that I might better understand that community's sense of faith, mission and ministry. Owanah Anderson's efforts help to share that part of our Church's history which has gone untold for far too long. As I have been able to learn the history of our Native American sisters and brothers through my visits at the Niobrara Convocation, at the Indian Convocations in Oklahoma and in Minnesota, and at urban centers, so, too, you will gain new insights of the richness and the poverty of our ministry among and with Native Americans in this book.

The Most Rev. Edmond L. Browning
Presiding Bishop, The Episcopal Church

Line drawings are by Willie Hillenbrand

© 1988. Forward Movement Publications,
412 Sycamore Street, Cincinnati, Ohio 45202

Contents

Appendices

The Rev. David Pendleton Oakerhater with his wife, Minnie White Buffalo (left) and his niece, Standing Twenty

Photo courtesy of Diocese of Oklahoma

About the Author

Born in Oklahoma, Owanah Anderson was reared on her Choctaw mother's 160-acre allotment in rural and wooded Choctaw County, surrounded by an extended family of aunts and cousins and headed by a diminutive but iron-willed grandmother who was rigidly Presbyterian. The missionaries had long ago scoured away much of the Choctaw traditions. Mrs. Anderson grew up in the pre-World War II era when Indians of Oklahoma had been so long oppressed that, in words of the Sioux author, Vine Deloria Jr., "they had come to accept this oppression as their lot in life. . ."

"The word 'oppression' wasn't in our vocabulary," said Mrs. Anderson, "but I can in retrospect recognize how this oppression affected our self-esteem. I remember how my grandmother wouldn't teach us the Choctaw language though it was spoken in her home and she, herself, had quite limited command of English. However, she shepherded us — a dozen cousins — to Choctaw language worship services at a rural Presbyterian mission called Pigeon Roost, so named because long ago the passenger pigeons came to roost among the black-jack oak trees which surrounded the little chapel. We sat on backless benches, under the stern scrutiny of our little grandmother, throughout Sunday mornings and far into the afternoons while a Choctaw preacher held forth interminably. We cousins understood scarcely a word he said. I remember her sad response to my wheedle to teach me the language. She said, 'Tain't no good. . .you study English hard, maybe so you grow up and be schoolteacher.' I wish she might have experienced the resurgence of pride in Indian identity among us today."

Heeding her grandmother's admonition, Mrs. Anderson did study hard and earned scholarships to the University of Oklahoma. Though she never became a school teacher, she sits on a committee for Harvard Graduate School of Education. Her professional career has been varied, ranging from media to business management, and she was deeply involved in social and women's issues on the national scene and in Texas, where she resided most of her adult life.

She became an Episcopalian after marriage to a committed churchman, a North Texas attorney who often said that one of the hardest jury arguments he ever delivered was to convince his wife to present herself at confirmation classes. Henry Joseph Anderson, a non-Indian, also influenced his wife to focus her considerable energies toward concerns of her own people. She founded and directed a national consortium of Native American professional women called "Ohoyo," which translates from the Choctaw simply as "woman." The consortium, funded by the U. S. Department of Education, published five books and held a series of national Indian women's leadership conferences.

"When my husband died in 1983, I was at a real crossroads. Our children

1

were then grown and didn't appear too eager to have a bossy grandmother telling them how to rear their young families. I knew I wanted to channel my energy in advocacy of Indian people and I held a deep commitment to my church. My diocesan bishop, the Rt. Rev. A. Donald Davies, encouraged me to merge the two driving interests, and in 1984, I ran away from hearth and home to New York City to head the Indian desk at Episcopal Church Center. Though I had never in my life lived alone and away from family, and I had certainly never lived in a city, I have somehow survived the culture shock."

Foreword

In the four hundred years of ministry among Native Americans, the Anglican Communion has not once had a definitive statement of the history of that ministry, and certainly not from the viewpoint of the people most directly touched by that ministry.

At last, a shameful blank in the history of the church has been filled, and filled admirably, by the present staff officer of Native American Ministry of the Episcopal Church. While this work is more of a series of sketches (in the words of the author) than an in-depth history, the reader will find far more valuable historical material in this volume that anywhere else in the published world.

To my knowledge, this is also the first work of church history to be written from the viewpoint and perspective of the people who were missionized (and often victimized) by those who "came to do good, and did very well." At the same time, the work reflects the many dedicated brothers and sisters of Christ, white and Indian, who labored long that the love of God might be shared among all people. Here you will meet saints and sinners, and so many who are in between. Here you will see the precious gift of the gospel, and the dreadful reality of human sin which often mars that gift. Here you will find the famous names of history, and those known only to God.

I do commend this volume to your study and enlightenment. In my prejudice, I would even commend it as required reading for those who would know the history of the Episcopal Church, and for those who would know the impact of the church, both for good and for ill, on the original inhabitants of this fair and God-blessed land.

As my own Seminole people would say, "Heyv nakokv heres." This book is good.

+William Eau Claire

AMERICAN INDIAN, ESKIMO & ALEUT
POPULATION OF THE UNITED STATES, 1980

Alabama	7,561	Montana	37,270
Alaska	64,047	Nebraska	9,197
Arizona	152,857	Nevada	13,304
Arkansas	9,411	New Hampshire	1,352
California	201,311	New Jersey	8,394
Colorado	18,059	New Mexico	104,777
Connecticut	4,533	New York	38,732
Delaware	1,330	North Carolina	64,635
District of Columbia	1,031	North Dakota	20,157
Florida	9,316	Ohio	12,240
Georgia	7,619	Oklahoma	169,464
Hawaii	2,778	Oregon	27,309
Idaho	10,521	Pennsylvania	9,459
Illinois	16,271	Rhode Island	2,898
Indiana	7,835	South Carolina	5,758
Iowa	5,453	South Dakota	45,101
Kansas	15,371	Tennessee	5,103
Kentucky	3,610	Texas	40,074
Louisiana	12,064	Utah	19,256
Maine	4,087	Vermont	984
Maryland	8,021	Virginia	9,336
Massachusetts	7,743	Washington	60,771
Michigan	40,038	West Virginia	1,610
Minnesota	35,026	Wisconsin	29,497
Mississippi	6,180	Wyoming	7,125
Missouri	12,319		

Preface

This volume does not presume to offer a comprehensive history of the English and American churches' Native American work; it offers, instead, **sketches** on how the work came about and where the work was at the end of the summer of 1987.

In oral histories of our various tribes, we each have our creation stories, a sense of origin being essential to our understanding of our time on earth. Therefore, the story here touches the "start" and the "now." It cannot cover the "in between."

The purpose of this volume is two-fold: to call the Episcopal Church to its commitment, assumed indirectly four centuries ago, to bring the gospel of Jesus Christ to peoples indigenous to the United States of America, and to tell of our own role as Indian people in response to the Great Commission.

This summer of 1987 marked the 400th anniversary of the first baptism of record of an American Indian by clergy of the Church of England. Though requirement was placed upon us to abandon our traditional values and lifestyle in order to become Christian, we responded in vast numbers to the message brought us by the "white robes" of the Episcopal Church. Yet, commitment is questioned when in the summer of 1987 we hear a plea from scattered and isolated Native American Episcopal congregations in the mountains and desert of the West, in areas where major mission once flourished and where a majority of reservation community had been confirmed Episcopalian, to "give us freedom from worry that the Episcopal Church will abandon us." One ponders evangelizing strategy and commitment when one reads in a 1985 study, Missions USA, that 92 per cent of today's Indians do not go to church. The study cites the Indians' need, as defined a few generations ago, for church to be the center of community life, and that this need goes unmet with clergy scarcity in rural and reservation communities, and even more so among those of us who have migrated to urban areas. The study underscores the fact that most Indians do not feel comfortable in inner city churches of the white, the black, or Hispanic. While Episcopal-baptized Indians are now residing in inner cities across the nation, less than a dozen Episcopal urban Indian congregations are organized.

A heretofore untold story has been the role of Native peoples in spreading the good news; a search of existing literature offers but fleeting, oblique glimpses of our cast of characters who moved about from place to place, tribe to tribe, to share the message the white man had brought about a holy man named Jesus, the Christ.

It is not my purpose to recite a litany of old grievances on Indian/white relations over the centuries; other Indian writers have ably addressed this protest. While I did not set out to unmask the myths surrounding church heroes

5

such as William Hobart Hare or Henry Benjamin Whipple, my views simply do not parallel the views of non-Native chroniclers of the past. Thus, in sketching our church's missionizing history among my people, I cannot with integrity avoid at times a confrontational posture. Racism and neglect have endured.

Records on American Indian work of the Episcopal Church have been ill-kept and ill-maintained. Scant was found in the Archives of the Episcopal Church in Austin, Texas, and chronicles of the early years of the National Committee on Indian Work were decidedly incomplete. Certain dioceses have included in their histories references to their Indian work; biographies of certain churchmen make mention of their Indian charges, but our place in their records can best be characterized as but incidental or addendum.

Since 1816, when the Episcopal Church founded its first American Indian mission, only three booklets offering an overview of Native American mission, all containing less than 100 pages, seem to have been published in 171 years of Episcopal evangelization, and the story has not previously been told from an Indian perspective.

The more comprehensive booklet is entitled *Indian Tribes and Missions: A Handbook of the General History of the North American Indians Early Missionary Efforts and Missions of the Episcopal Church.* It was written in 1925, updated in 1934, and published by Church Missions Publishing Company, Hartford, Connecticut. Its language is patronizing; its coverage is inconceivably inadequate on the role of American Indians to the mission endeavor. Enmegahbowh was accorded half a page though this man was the first Native American ordained to the priesthood and largely responsible for the founding of the mother mission of Indian work west of the Mississippi.

A shorter work is entitled *On the Trail to Tomorrow,* published by the National Council Church Missions House in New York. No date is listed; no author is listed. However, noting that the price was listed at 15 cents, one would surmise it was published long, long ago. David Pendleton Oakerhater, the deacon saint of Oklahoma, is dismissed with: "In 1884 two Indian **boys,** who had been educated in New York, were ordained deacons and returned west with a missionary priest to minister to Cheyennes and Kiowas." David Oakerhater was at least 35 years old when ordained and would be the only Episcopal clergy presence in all of Indian Territory for 12 years.

The third short work, published in 1955, is written with more sensitivity. Also published by the National Council, *The Trail Ahead,* lists Varian H. Cassat as author. It sold for 75 cents.

Certain available source materials, such as the old Episcopal periodical, Spirit of Missions, were written in a perspective repugnant to an Indian person in 1987. Frequently in tedious research through these materials, I found it necessary to close the files and walk away, questioning at times my own

6

commitment to an institution whose history, as reflected in the language of its old publications, was so brazenly patronizing and racist. Then I would remind myself of lines of Herman Melville asserting that "Missionary undertaking — however blessed in Heaven — is in itself but human, and subject like everything else to frailty and abuse." So, I resumed research. More significantly, I could seize upon the hope and brighter promises ahead as barriers are burned and Native Americans are admitted, at last, to full partnership in the life and decision-making tier of the Episcopal Church.

New vision in mission and ministry with Native Americans is being crafted. There is brighter promise. The 24th Presiding Bishop of the Episcopal Church, the Most Rev. Edmond L. Browning, proclaimed to us at a major consultation in Oklahoma in October 1986: "We are partners in the mission and ministry of this church, equally called by Christ to proclaim the good news to all creation."

As the mission imperatives of the Browning era, projected to extend to the eve of the 21st century, unfold, Episcopal-confirmed Native Americans envision last rites for the centuries-old paternalistic missionary mold through which church and state collaborated in ritualistic, near-successful assimilation policies and programs.

New ministry is developing, especially in urban settings. Our church was indeed slow to follow the American Indian as we migrated, generally out of economic necessity, from our reservations or traditional homelands into urban areas. In 1984 there was but one growing and thriving Episcopal urban Indian worshiping community which was accorded diocesan-wide focus and support. This was the work in the Twin Cities, in the Diocese of Minnesota. By the summer of 1987 new urban congregations were stabilized in Albuquerque, Denver and Portland; new promise was emerging in other western cities; new and renewed interest in the middle west and northern plains. The past year has seen a new model in Native American leadership development materialize at Seabury-Western Theological Seminary in Evanston, Illinois. Province of the Pacific had strengthened its Indian Commission. New mutual-support coalitions had been launched and include a regional grouping in the interior west, a Native clergy and an urban Indian network.

As brighter promises evolve from new strategies in mission and ministry **with** Native Americans, and as we, ourselves, define our role in an inclusive church, it is essential to review how the gospel of Jesus Christ was brought by the American/Episcopal Church to our people.

A vast segment of Episcopal communicants know virtually nothing about the Episcopal Church's past and current ministry among us. Nor is there broad understanding about us as contemporary beings, or about our various tribes' unique relationship — the treaty/trust relationship — with the U. S. government, or about the native spirituality of our many and varied cultures. Bishop

William Wantland of Eau Claire has termed this lack of an informational base as an "ignorance of ignorance."

Contemporary beings:

Ongoing is our problem of calling the dominant society to the reality that we are contemporary beings and should not be viewed as relics of the past, museum pieces, or a "vanished" people. According to the U. S. Bureau of Census — and many Indians charge an undercount — in 1980 we numbered approximately one and one-half million. We are a growing population; the 1980 census showed a whopping 73 per cent population increase over the previous decade, whether by a better system of enumeration or by birth increase, it is not known. A century ago, in the period of the "vanishing American" image, it was believed that less than 250,000 of us had survived European-imported epidemics, "Indian wars," loss of the traditional way of life including food supply, and federally-instituted reservation systems.

We did not vanish. Roughly 35,000, or two percent of us, are baptized-Episcopalian.

Our often patronizing non-Indian pew mates seem to be able in a feeble effort to understand us to get no further than asking what we prefer to be called: American Indian, Native American, or what. No Indian person presumes to speak for all Indians; therefore, I can speak only for myself. It simply does not matter. We were misnamed at the onset, and in an ineffectual effort to rectify a 500-year-old error, scholars of a generation ago decided we should be called Native Americans. An advantage to the "Native American" identification is that it can include Native Alaskans, some of whom are not classified as American Indian; the disadvantage is that any person born in this country is a native of America. Among ourselves, we identify by our tribal membership. I am a Choctaw and think of myself as such; it bothers me not one whit to be called an Indian.

Unique Relationship with U.S. Government:

The least understood factor about us is our tribes' unique relationship with the government of the United States, and this factor alone will never allow us to be simply deposited into that great grouping called "minorities."

As other ethnic minorities demanded civil rights, we spoke to legal rights, rights bought and paid for with land. The church must still, however, be frequently reminded that the government of the United States entered into honorable and legal agreements with our many tribes and nations which are in effect in perpetuity. Some Indians suggest that the sense of dispiritedness and hopelessness which exists in some of our communities springs from the grief syndrome; we have never recovered from the loss of our land. Some 650 treaties were made in exchange for the land, the heart of this nation. The United States agreed in many of these treaties to provide our tribes and nations with certain special rights in exchange for the land. These treaties are, in effect, old real estate transactions; we need the church's continuing help in collecting our mortgage payments. We have no power to evict.

Socio-economic status of the American Indian/Alaskan Native is, and continues to be, at the lowest rung on any indicator. We have the shortest life span, greatest infant mortality, lowest annual income, highest unemployment rate, highest rates of alcoholism, diabetes and tuberculosis of any ethnic group of the land. Many of these deplorable conditions result directly from the failure of the government of the United States to live up to its treaty obligations, such as providing treaty-obligated health care.

Despite these statistics, we choose to erase the "Lo the poor Indian" image. The barrels of old clothing dispatched to distant Indian missions — a frequent benevolent outpouring of the past — is not now the need. There is need for companion relationships of affluent parishes with Indian chapels and clergy, which should be coordinated through diocesan offices or constituency-designated members of the National Committee on Indian work.

Of great importance to our survival is for the communicants of the Episcopal Church to stand highly visible in support of our tribal rights. In the last decade when Indian court claims have been upheld — fishing and hunting rights in the Pacific Northwest and in Wisconsin; land claims of the Great Sioux Nation — there was a backlash against Indians and powerful anti-treaty groups surfaced. These groups have called for abrogation of "old and outdated" Indian treaties. We Indians ask: should the U.S. Constitution be thrown away simply because it is 200 years old?

Because of the seriousness of this new era of hostility toward Indian people, included as appendix II of this volume is a paper written by a Seminole attorney, the Rt. Rev. William Wantland, Bishop of Eau Claire. Bishop Wantland's paper contains the Treaty Rights Resolution adopted by the 1985 Anaheim General Convention which calls the Episcopal Church to support and honor Indian treaty rights.

Native spirituality:

Non-Indians in the past few years have articulated much interest in Native spirituality. Many Indian Episcopalians are still trying to sort out whether this interest stems from a search for foundational direction in a fractured world, or if this interest is but another fad or pell-mell rush to instant insight.

There is no consensus definition of Native American spirituality among the native populations or among Native American Christians. A 12-member, predominantly-Indian, Episcopal task force recently deliberated at length on how to communicate Native spirituality to the broader church. There was consensus that it is essential to distinguish between the ceremonial and the spiritual as well as the underlying principles which separate practices and beliefs.

The task force cited danger in allowing the non-Indian world to perceive that Native spirituality translates only into the ceremonial aspects — the sweat lodge, pipe ceremony, sweet grass — and agreed that the message which must be conveyed to the non-Native church is the native concept of non-compartmentalization which holds there to be no separation between the secular and the sacred. The group called for a building of awareness of the totality of God's presence and of all life being related.

It was also agreed that the church must affirm that the spiritual truths held by our forbearers are not worthless and evil.

A major Episcopal consultation on Native American ministry, held in 1986, issued a document called "The Covenant of Oklahoma II" which is included as appendix VIII. The covenant calls for the exposure of the whole church to Native spirituality, and the encouraging of native communities to offer this spirituality to the whole church.

The Choctaw Episcopal priest, scholar and educator, Steve Charleston, refers to Native spirituality as our cultures' Old Testament. He is in process of publishing new work on the native Christian theology, a work forthcoming shortly. We appreciate permission of Forward Movement for allowing reprint as appendix III of a previous work of Fr. Charleston on Native spirituality.

The Episcopal Church's Present Ministry Among Native Americans

Frequent are telephone calls and letters to the desk of Native American Ministries at Episcopal Church Center in New York inquiring about the church's present ministry among American Indians and Alaskan Natives.

There is some sort of specialized Indian work going on in approximately one-third of the 98 Episcopal dioceses in the United States. Some of the work is limited to a single predominantly-Indian congregation within the dioceses; some is an exciting new urban Indian ministry; some dioceses, such as South Dakota, have major and comprehensive Native American work. A diocese by diocese survey of present Indian work is included as appendix IV.

It was difficult to exclude from this publication sketches on former Episcopal Indian mission. The old *Spirit of Missions* publications informed of work, which ceased long ago, among the Seminole in Florida, the Karok in California and the Havasupai in Arizona. It was especially hard not to include the ill-fated Ponca, to whom Episcopal mission came in 1871. A young deacon from Maryland "came out" and during his first year baptized 29, but by 1877 the Ponca, on advice of Bishop William Hobart Hare, were unwillingly removed from the Northern plains to the Quapaw Agency in Indian Territory (Oklahoma) and the Episcopal Church did not accompany the Ponca southward. It was tempting to include a sketch on a forgotten mission on the St. Regis Mohawk Reservation in upper New York state; all that remains is an overgrown and neglected cemetery with an historical marker proclaiming that at this spot originally was buried an Episcopal clergyman, the Rev. Eleazar Williams, "who claimed to be the son of Louis XVI of France."

Much is missing. American Indians were not writing the chronicles during the westward movement. But if the sketches contained herein on the Turtle Mountain Chippewa, Rising Sun, found and cherished like a treasure that the sea washed up, proves to be an inspiration to one young person on a Dakota reservation, the effort will have been worthwhile.

I extend very special appreciation to two authors for permission to quote most liberally from their publications: Virginia Driving Hawk Sneve for *That They May Have Life: The Episcopal Church in South Dakota, 1859-1976* and Tay Thomas for *Cry in the Wilderness* in the Alaska section.

Lastly, I acknowledge with much appreciation the many Indians and non-Indians who encouraged and championed, challenged and cajoled me toward completion this work. Among these were the Creek scholar, Blue Clark of Oklahoma; Alaska clergy who shared collected remembrances; Alice Emery, former executive of National Mission in Church and Society, who helped fill in gaps in the records of the last decades; Helen Peterson, my mentor; Caddo scholar, Carol Hampton who emphasized need for the volume; Rosella Jom and Bishop Wes Frensdorff, whose review and comment assured accuracy in the Navajo section; Howard Anderson and my son, Steven, who insisted the chronicle from an Indian perspective must be written. For their contributed pieces to the volume, I thank three distinguished Indian Churchmen: Bishop Harold Jones (Sioux), Bishop William Wantland (Seminole) and Fr. Steve Charleston (Choctaw). And, I extend personal appreciation to Clint Best who befriended, encouraged, and contributed to my spiritual growth when I arrived in 1984 from the distant West to head the "Indian desk" in the alien and lonely world of Manhattan Island.

Owanah Anderson
Choctaw

New York City
September 1, 1987
Feast day: David Pendleton Oakerhater,
deacon saint of Oklahoma

**Cornelius Hill was the first
Oneida ordained priest.**

Chapter 1

How it all began

James I occupied the throne of England; the year was 1606. At some royal palace in distant London, the King of England set his seal upon the charter which would establish Jamestown Colony and, thereupon, trigger cultural genocide for people indigenous to America.

A royal ordinance accompanying the Jamestown Charter irrevocably proclaimed a commitment of the Church of England to mission and ministry among American Indians:

> . . . *the true word of God be preached, planted and used not only in the colonies, but also as much as might be, among the savages bordering upon them, and this according to the rites and doctrines of the Church of England.*

Thus the Anglican commitment to preach and plant the true word of God among the American Indians was firmly established with the first permanent English settlement in America.

The 1607 Jamestown settlers were not, of course, the first to bring the gospel of Jesus Christ to the western hemisphere; the Spanish and the French, under the flags of the Roman Catholic Church, antedated the English protestants by generations.

When European explorers, adventurers and missionaries arrived in what would become the continental United States of America there were at least 300 functioning societies of native peoples, each speaking distinctively different languages and each with different cultures, histories and relationships with a Creator.

Exploitation of the riches of the "new world" and slavery of its inhabitants immediately came with European contact. Though European sovereigns stoutly stated intentions "to gather millions of wandering heathen souls into the fold of Christ," timing of the "age of discovery" could not have been worse from the vantage point of native peoples of the western world. Political strife colored the whole of Europe and conflicts depleted royal treasuries. Protestants were leaving the Roman Church in large numbers. Spain, throwing off Moorish domination after almost eight centuries, embarked into the odious era of inquisition, and anyone who did not readily profess catholicism was automatically considered less than human.

There was, in fact, theological debate across Europe as to whether Indians were indeed human. It was questioned whether, if Indians were unknown to biblical and classical authorities, they were part of the human race at all. It was almost half a century after the first voyage of Christopher Columbus

13

that Pope Paul III in 1537 issued a papal bull declaring that Indians were indeed "true men."

Nonetheless, conversion of the Natives was declared to be the prime objective of the second voyage of Columbus. Six priests were sent along to accomplish it. However, the voyage, in 1494, also established a colony on the island of Hispaniola, and within two decades enslaved Indians were working the Spanish mines and plantations and dying by the thousands. These Indians had innocently welcomed Columbus in 1492. By 1515 the native population on this fertile island had shrunk from an estimated quarter of a million to around 14,000, and in a few more years, the native population would be extinct.

A wealthy Dominican friar was among the first to accept as a religious duty to influence the Spanish government to amend its cruel and inhuman treatment of the native peoples. He was Bartholomew de las Casas, born in Seville, who journeyed to America in 1502, took holy orders in 1510, and became the first Roman Catholic priest ordained in the new world. He was appalled by the exploitation of the Indians and labored through his long life to ameliorate the situation. He was also a historian and left behind insightful observations:

> *God created these simple people without evil and without guile.*
> *They are most submissive, patient, peaceful and virtuous. Nor are*
> *they quarrelsome, rancorous, querulous, or vengeful. Moreover they*
> *are more delicate than princes and die easily from work or illness.*
> *They neither possess nor desire to possess worldly wealth. Surely*
> *these people would be the most blessed in the world if only they wor-*
> *shiped the true God.*

Russian fur expeditions sprinkled Orthodox missions along the west coast during the Russian imperial expansion. Holland spread limited numbers of Dutch Reformed native converts through southern New England, while Swedish missionaries founded Lutheran Indian settlements outward from Delaware Bay after 1638. Early French colonizing efforts were sporadic; missionizing efforts were primarily among the nations of the powerful Iroquois Confederacy in the present state of New York. There had been in 1562 an unsuccessful effort to establish a colony of French Huguenots on the coast of South Carolina, but previous encounters with the Spanish made the Indians afraid and unaccepting. The French influence among the Iroquois left a tangled skein to be dealt with in several ensuing colonial wars. It has been said that had not the Iroquois sided with the British, we all might be speaking French today.

Chapter 2

Missions of the Church of England

Anglican/Episcopal endeavor toward bringing the good news of Jesus Christ to native peoples of America is a saga spilling across more than 400 years, from 1579 when the gospel was first preached by an Anglican priest before an assembly of American Indians; 1587 when the Church of England baptized its first Indian convert; 1606 when the Jamestown Charter specified that "the true word of God be preached and planted among the savages."

With protestant zeal, the English prayer book, and the King James Bible, men of Britain by the mid-1600s had institutionalized a mission model fraught with ethnocentrism, cultural imperialism and ecclesiastical colonialism.

Native peoples of the western hemisphere first heard the gospel preached by clergy of the Church of England not along the eastern seaboard, so closely identified with Anglican influence, but at a "fayre and good baye" on the mist-shrouded coast of northern California. It was the year 1579, on or about St. John the Baptist's Day. Instrument to the event was the unlikely "freebooter," Sir Francis Drake. His chaplain, the Rev. Francis Fletcher, held services for the ship's crew, and history provides a fleeting glimpse of "a large company of Indians gathered to see the newcomers."

William Stevens Perry, bishop of Iowa, in 1885 produced a two-volume work, The History of the American Episcopal Church: 1587 — 1882. He described the Drake encounter:

> *In the presence of the aborigines of this distant land, these rough sailors, who scrupled not to plunder or murder every Spaniard they met, lifted their eyes and hands to heaven, to indicate by these symbolic gestures that God is over all; and then, following their chaplain's lead, they besought their God, in the Church's prayers, to reveal himself to these idolaters and to open their blinded eyes to the knowledge of Him and of Jesus Christ, the salvation of the Gentiles.*

Roanoke, the Lost Colony

By tradition, the first Indian convert to the Church of England was Manteo, chieftain on Roanoke Island, present-day North Carolina, and site of the first English settlement in North America. In 1584, Sir Walter Raleigh began attempts to establish a permanent colony and his explorers scouted the area at the entrance of Albermarle Sound. They returned to England with reports that the area was

> *...the most plentiful, sweet, fruitful, and wholesome of all the world; unspoiled natives such as live after the manner of the golden age...*

15

Manteo accompanied the scouting party back to England where he was again to visit a few years later, hitching a ride with Sir Francis Drake who stopped by Roanoke after one of his raids in the Spanish West Indies.

Known in history as the Lost Colony, the 108 Roanoke settlers set forth from Plymouth on Good Friday, 1585. Queen Elizabeth I, who deemed that the "new" land be called Virginia, in the first charter for an English colony provided for the recognition of

> . . .the honor of God and his compassion for the poor infidels, it seeming probable that God hath reserved these Gentiles to be introduced into Christian civility by the English nation.

The queen's then-favorite courtier, Sir Walter, waved the settlers off as they transported one hundred pounds of sterling to be applied in planting the Christian religion, and advancing the same. Thus, it was Sir Walter Raleigh who provided the first Anglican gift of record for the evangelizing of the American shores.

Lost in time has been the full manifest of passengers on the seven vessels which set sail for Virginia. Unquestionably among the passengers were clergy of the Church of England. It is recorded that Manteo was "on the 13th of August, 1587, admitted to Christ's Church by Holy Baptism." This first ecclesiastical act of record was followed one week later with the christening of Virginia Dare, the first English child born in America.

Having claim to being the first English missionary to the Indians is Thomas Heriot, the mathematician, who spent a year at the Roanoke settlement. He is best remembered, however, as inventor of the system of notation used in modern algebra. While at Roanoke, Heriot roamed the vicinity making careful notes on vegetation, including the potato and the "many and rare virtues" of the tobacco plant. His notes, preserved by Richard Hakluyt, prebendary of Westminister, inform of Heriot's travels to Indian villages where he told the natives as best he could of the doctrine of salvation through Christ.

The ill-fated Roanoke colony was established at the height of the reign of Elizabeth, at a time, described by Bishop Perry, when:

> . . .the spirit of adventure was rife in England; and the zeal for evangelization of the heathen beyond the sea animated the English Church and the realm. . .

The colony, however, was abandoned for three years while England faced the Spanish Armada. When the supply ships finally returned, the settlement had vanished. The single clue, carved on a tree, was the word CROATOAN, the place where Manteo was born. A century later, Hatteras Indians of the Croatoan area were "wont to tell that several of their ancestors were white people, and the truth of which may be affirmed by gray eyes being frequently found among these Indians." Thirty thousand Lumbee Indians, today living in rural North Carolina, allude to descent from the Lost Colony settlers.

Jamestown: The first permanent English settlement

Bearing the King's command to preach "among the savages... according to the rites and doctrines of the church of England," the Jamestown party arrived on the American mainland on April 2, 1607. The first report filed back to England described flowers of diverse colors and fine and beautiful strawberries "foure times bigger and better than ours in England." A report dated Whitsunday, May 24, informs of "kindly intercourse with the savages at a banquet to which their chieftain, Powhatan, had been an invited guest." A description of the people in this very early account gives a fleeting recognition of the Native spirituality:

> ...I find they account after death to goe into another world, pointing eastward...To conclude, they are a very witty and ingenious people, apt both to understand and speake our language. So that I hope in God, as he hath miraculously preserved us from all dangers both of sea and land and their fury, so he will make us authors of his holy will in converting them to our true Christian faith.

The best remembered convert of the first English permanent settlement was the chieftain's daughter, Pocahontas. Her romanticized story about saving Captain John Smith needs no retelling. Powhatan was chief of a strong confederacy of the James River tribes. Neglecting rudimentary corn planting the first season, the English would have starved had it not been for the support of the Indians. During those first crucial years, Powhatan, at any time, could have eliminated the English settlement. Afterward, more English arrived and seized more land, giving rise to friction, and the Indians decided too late to sweep away the white intruders.

The "Princess" Pocahontas — the English penchant for superimposing trappings of European nobility surfaced early — was being held hostage aboard an English ship at anchor in the James River at the time she was admitted to Holy Baptism. "Foure honest and learned Ministers," among them Alexander Whitaker, had arrived in the colony in May, 1611. According to Bishop Perry's research, the Rev. Mr. Whitaker, accorded the title of "Apostle of Virginia," prepared Pocahontas for Holy Baptism, whereupon she took the name of Rebecca:

> Detained, with a view to secure from her father the return of men and stores which he had in possession, Pocahontas learned to love her captors... (she) renounced publickly her countrey Idolatry (and) was as she desired baptized.

Her marriage to the widower John Rolfe was solemnized in the little church at Jamestown, and her family members present included two brothers and an uncle. The date of her marriage, April 1, 1613, has puzzled scholars, considering the church's aversion to weddings during Lent. The first day of April in 1613 was Maundy Thursday. About three years later, Pocahontas accompanied her husband to England where she was received, under the name of Lady Rebecca, in pomp and state by Kings James, his queen, and the Bishop of London. As she prepared to return to Virginia in the winter of 1616, "she came to Grauesend, to her end and graue," at age 22, leaving one infant son.

While the Pocahontas-Rolfe union is among the best remembered events of the Jamestown Settlement, it is interesting to note that one William Symonds in a sermon delivered in 1609 at St. Savior's, Southwark, threatened the wrath of God upon any Englishman who might take an Indian maid as his wife.

The Symonds sermon, along with several pontifical discourses of other clergy back in England, has been preserved in tracts circulated for the purpose of gaining financial support for the colony. These tracts, rife with anti-Roman bias, underscore a mission to establish a protestant "bulwark against the Papists." There is assertion that "the eyes of all Europe are looking upon our endeavors to spread the Gospell among the heathen people of Virginia."

This mission, however, seems propelled more by greed than grace. Robert Gray voiced a position that the settlers should consider it their divine right to "caste out the Canaanites." God gave the Englishmen Virginia; let them take it. Gray did, however, reason that it was better to convert the heathen than put him to the sword, "if the land can then be taken peacefully."

In 1619 the first legislative assembly of American colonists met in the "Quire of the Church in James City" and set forth brief declaration of purpose to include "Conversion of the Savages." Out of this assembly came specific directions for establishment of a "University and Colledge" for the sons of settlers and for the education of Indian children. Sir Edwyn Sandys, treasurer for the Virginia Company, was instrumental in setting aside a vast land grant for Henrico College for the "education of the children of the Barbarian." A fund-raising drive was mounted in England; the Bishop of London collected a thousand pounds toward Henrico College. However, by 1622, a new trend would emerge which precluded further efforts toward either education or conversion of the aborigines. The year 1622 brought the Indian "uprising." Thenceforth, Indian policy of the Virginians would be extermination. Bishop Perry's account of the 1622 event contains this addendum:

> ...the Massacre would have been complete had it not been for a Christian Indian. Solicited the night before the outbreak by his own brother to engage in the fiendish plot, the faithful convert found means to acquaint his master with the impending danger.

18

So, the University of Henrico was never to be built and the clergy and colonists in Virginia "lost heart with respect to the advancement of Christian education, or the bringing of the natives to the faith and Church of Christ." Years would elapse before any attempt would be renewed.

Records of the colonial period reveal that no real systematic effort was made to convert the great southern Indian nations. A bland admission to the lack of response to the Great Commission is found in Indian Tribes and Mission: A Handbook of Early Missionary Efforts, published in 1925 by Church Missions Publishing Company, Hartford, Connecticut. Though the prevailing obdurate tone of the work is unacceptable to 20th century American Indians, this Episcopal publication confesses the sin of omission thusly:

As a rule, the Indian was left to be the prey of the trader and adventurer, and to learn the vices, and not the virtues, of the race which drove him further and further into the wilderness, and took possession of his lands, sometimes by purchase and more often by conquest.

Other literature of the southern colonial period provides a preface to subsequent acculturation processes and policies of the new republic of the United States designed to mold the Indian into a brown replica of the European conqueror.

One illustrative story out of the colonial period which today's Indian scholars relish the telling of concerns a generous bequest left to William and Mary College by a wealthy member of the Virginia gentry to educate Indians. The college trustees set out recruiting; the distant Seneca of the north were contacted and offered education for six of their young men. The Seneca chiefs replied with a masterful, yet-quoted message which underscores yet-relevant cultural values:

We know that you highly esteem the kind of learning taught in those colleges. But, you who are wise must know that the different nations have different conceptions of things; and you will not, therefore, take it amiss if our ideas of this kind of education happen not to be the same with yours.

Several of our young men were formerly brought up at the colleges of the northern provinces; they were instructed in all your sciences; but when they came back to us they were bad runners, ignorant of every means of living in the woods, unable to bear either cold or hunger, knew neither how to build a cabin, take a deer or kill an enemy; spoke our language imperfectly — they were, therefore, neither fit for hunters, warriors nor counselors. They were totally good for nothing.

We are, therefore, not the less obliged by your kind offer, though we decline the accepting of it; and, to show our grateful sense of it, if the gentlemen of Virginia will send us a dozen of their sons, we will take care to their education, instruct them in all that we know, and make men of them.

Jamestown legacy: Episcopal southern mission neglect

Eastern and southern Indian nations suffered the brunt of the European's insatiable greed for land. The early 1800s were marked by the sweeping missionary movement. Missions in distant lands were zealously pursued by the emerging Episcopal Church once it reorganized itself in an independent status following the American Revolution.

The young church, however, was unconscionably mute while Andrew Jackson's removal policy herded the great Indian nations of the south — Choctaw, Chickasaw, Cherokee, Seminole and Creek — westward on the "Trail of Tears." Episcopal churchmen of Dixieland dug deeply into their pockets to evangelize on distant continents, but largely ignored the neighboring remnants of Native peoples.

The Episcopal Church was otherwise occupied when American Board of Commissioners for Foreign Parts (ABCFM) was formed in 1810, primarily spearheaded by Presbyterians and Congregationalists, as a major missionary movement among American Indians. The Episcopal Church was still going through the throes of internal grounding when, for instance, Presbyterian missionaries walked westward in the early 1830s from the deltas of Mississippi to distant Indian Territory (Oklahoma) with 18,000 peaceable Choctaw, a forced march during which 6,000 Choctaw perished.

The Episcopal Church was silent when the ABCFM missionaries were instruments to a major Supreme Court decision, cited yet as landmark in Indian law. The ABCFM missionary, Samuel Worcester, was principal in the 1832 decision, *Worcester* v. *Georgia,* which held the Cherokee nation to be a sovereign nation, and therefore not subject to the laws of the state of Georgia. President Andrew Jackson, who tenaciously championed the Removal Act, ignored the court decision saying, "Mr. Chief Justice Marshall has made his decision; now let us see him enforce it." Removal went on.

Today, across the whole of the south, where the Episcopal Church enjoys major communicant strength, there are only two American Indian Episcopal missions — St. Paul's among the near-forgotten Monacans in Amherst County, Virginia, and St. Anna's among the Poarch Band of Creek Indians in Escambia County, Alabama, in the Diocese of Central Gulf Coast.

The forgotten Monacans of Virginia

The "forgotten" Monacans are of Siouan stock, left behind, it is believed, when the nomadic Sioux wandered for generations across the south and east.

First European contact was made by none other than Captain John Smith, who in 1608 sent a company of 120 men up the James River into the foothills of the Blue Ridge Mountains.

Through the centuries the Monacans were viewed as different from their neighbors, the Cherokee, the Algonquins, and other coastal Indians. It was strongly suggested that the Monacans mixed with Tuscaroras who remained behind when the main body moved in the 1700s from the Carolinas homeland to join their kindred of the Iroquois Confederacy in New York state.

There was early caucasian mixture among the Monacans, who late in the last century were "discovered" living in isolation on Bear Mountain near the locale described by the Smith expedition of almost 300 years before. Likely, there had been black mixture; a "settlement" of freed black slaves had long been established on the opposite side of Bear Mountain. Considerable tension, however, was long noted between the people who "looked like Indians" and their neighbors who were descendants of freed slaves. The term "free issue" initially applied to slaves given freedom before the Civil War. However, it became inclusive, and the Indian mountain people despised identification as "issues." Furthermore, the Indians refused to attend black schools. They were not allowed in white schools. The Indians refused black medical facilities, nor would they worship at black churches.

Episcopal mission arrived among the Monacans in 1907. A young seminarian, Arthur Gray Jr., dreamed of going to Japan as a missionary. His father, rector of Ascension Church in nearby Amherst, encouraged his son to look closer to home for mission work. A descendant of Virginia gentry, young Gray during the summer between gradation from the University of Virginia and entry into Alexandria Theological Seminary was able to acquire land and raise $1,500 to build the mission church and school for the Monacans on Bear Mountain.

For the next half-century, the Monacan mission was run by a series of devoted deaconesses, the last of which was the indomitable Florence Cowan, who in the 1950s led the challenge on school integration on behalf of Monacan children.

In 1965 the Church Army came to Bear Mountain mission and for three years Captain Robert Hicks served the Monacan congregation. He was followed by Captain John Haraughty, a native of western Oklahoma, who knew well insidious racism as it related to American Indians. Captain Haraughty continues the battle in the foothills of the Blue Ridge Mountains to break down old barriers that restricted a racially, socially, and culturally isolated group of American Indians from medical, educational, and housing opportunities available in the mainstream of 20th century American life.

St. Anna's among the Eastern Creeks

In 1929 Edgar Van W. Edwards, priest in charge of Trinity Mission, Atmore,

Alabama, reported to Bishop William G. McDowell that there were many in the Poarch Indian community centered in the Perdido Hills area that he believed were "unchurched." The bishop replied, "Then, see if you can round them up and we will try to start a mission." Fr. Edwards made house-to-house calls among the Creek Indians who had long lived in near obscurity in rural Escambia County, remaining behind when the main body of the nation had been removed in the 1830s to Indian Territory (Oklahoma). The priest disclosed that he would preach in the little one-room school house on a specified night. The night came; Fr. Edwards came; no one else came. This happened several times.

Finally, Fr. Edwards was informed that before any of the tribesmen would respond the minister would have to see Acting Chief Fred Walker (the real chief, Aleck Rolin, was around 100 and very feeble; Walker had been elected acting chief). Fr. Edwards called on Chief Walker and was given permission to preach and the first service saw the little school house packed, with many standing outside. Encouraged by the response, the bishop shortly sent a medical missionary and his wife, a United Thank Offering volunteer, to minister to the many medical ills of the Alabama Creeks. Dr. and Mrs. R. C. Macy, who had served as missionaries in Mexico, offered health care and treatment to all the Indians in Escambia County who then made a living as sharecroppers, small farmers, migrant farm laborers and unskilled laborers in timber and turpentine industries.

The first Episcopal baptism was that of the beloved Chief Aleck Rolin, a few days before he died. By the end of the first year of the mission, 50 were enrolled in Sunday school and eight were ready for baptism. Baptism was by immersion — immersion was the only way the Indians knew and accepted. Bishop McDowell promptly appeared for confirmation. Another "first" of that year was an Episcopal wedding — of the new chief's daughter, Ruby Walker, and Alfred Jackson.

In less than three years, there were two church buildings, built entirely by the Creeks in the middle of the depression. The first was St. John's-in-the-Wilderness, and three miles away was the second chapel, St. Anna's, named by the Indians to honor Mrs. Macy who had been widowed during the year previous but chose to stay on to assist with the mission. Both church buildings doubled as schools.

For 18 years, the Episcopal churches provided virtually all the education available to around 600 Creek Indians residing near the Florida border in Escambia County, Alabama. Since the turn of the century, Indians had been excluded from the rural county's white schools, and the county provided no schools for the Indians. The Episcopal schools offered elementary education but the Indian children were not permitted to ride the white school buses into Atmore for junior and high school. It was not until after World War II that the Poarch Indians rose in protest, and stood in the middle of the road to stop the high school bound bus, threatened lawsuit against the county school board, and eventually saw reform and access to public education.

In the mid-1940s, St-John's-in-the-Wilderness closed. St. Anna's has continued for more than a half-century. On two occasions, St. Anna's was visited by the distinguished Sioux priest, the Ven. Vine Deloria Sr., and through the years various Episcopal Church workers provided the Poarch Band of Creek Indians with many social and education services as well as spiritual guidance.

With roots in the first Episcopal mission among the eastern Creeks is Buford Rolin, former officer of National Committee on Indian Work of the Episcopal Church. An officer for the oldest national Indian organization, National Congress of American Indians, Rolin is a lay leader in the Diocese of Central Gulf Coast which was formed in 1971 and includes the region of the once-isolated Poarch Creeks. The diocese in 1983 demonstrated its ongoing commitment to American Indian ministry through designation of Venture in Mission funding of $190,000 to assist with seminary education of Native American clergy.

Hobart Church, built in 1825 on the Oneida Resevation in Wisconsin, named for New York's Bishop John Henry Hobart

23

Harold S. Jones, first American Indian bishop

Chapter 3

The New England scene: Setting lasting patterns in Native mission

From the rugged shores of New England sprang the blueprint for bringing the gospel to the Indian, and from this design, shaped by the mid-1600s, there came the mission model which would prevail well into the 20th century. The model was fraught with ethnocentrism, cultural imperialism and ecclesiastical colonialism.

Charters for establishment of the New England colonies were virtual replicas of the Jamestown Charter, specifying evangelization of the Indian as a principal purpose. A difference, however, was that the New England colonies would shortly set out with zeal and fervor to bring the gospel, and they determined early the pattern and policy by which the gospel would be brought.

Ethnocentrism was crystallized in the efforts of John Eliot who came to be known as the "Apostle to the Indians." The Roxbury minister brought the conviction that it was essential to "civilize" as well as to evangelize the Indian. Thus, conditions were placed upon Indians as a prerequisite to conversion. Indians must desert their cultures, social structures, their people, and all vestiges of their traditional religion, and, in fact, speak, act, and dress like the western European in order to "walk the Jesus road."

Cultural imperialism was decreed by law in 1644 when a Massachusetts governing body prohibited Indians — on threat of death — from "paw-pawing" or performing worship to false gods. The same law makers also decreed the death penalty for any Indian who blasphemed God or the Christian religion.

New England missionaries exemplified ecclesiastical colonialism when they extracted the Indian from his tribal life and established him in mission towns. From the outset in Indian and white relationships, the land was at stake. The mission towns of Christian or "praying" Indians would effectively reduce land use by the Native people while at the same time serving as an agent to "civilize" the Indian. This pattern later evolved into the reservation system, a policy favored two centuries later by another churchman known as "Apostle to the Indians."

Though the Connecticut colony appeared more concerned about compelling the Indians to keep the Sabbath than anything else, the rest of New England took seriously the command of the King of England to serve as "instruments of spreading the Gospel of Christ among the heathen Nationes."

Other ministers would toil in the mission field — Roger Williams among the Narraganset, the Mayhew father and son among the Wampanoag on Martha's Vineyard and Nantucket, Richard Bourne among the Mashpee on Cape Cod — but it was John Eliot who is best remembered.

Beginning his Indian work in 1649, Eliot continued until his death in 1695. He learned the Algonquin language and began to preach. He translated the Bible and had it printed at the Indian college he established in Harvard Yard. He was largely responsible for establishing the towns of "praying" Indians, and by 1674 there were 14 such towns with populations totaling 4,000. He spearheaded efforts to establish seminaries to train Indians as teachers and preachers, and by 1700, at a point of decline after "King Philip's War," there were 37 Indian preachers in the field working along with seven or eight English ministers. This ratio has never again been attained.

Metacom or Philip — dubbed King Philip by the English — was a grandson of Massasoit, the Wampanoag chief who had come with 90 men to celebrate the first Thanksgiving with the Pilgrims. Philip is recorded to have stated to an Englishman:

> *But little remains of my ancestors' domain; I am resolved not to see the day when I have no country. . .The English are so eager to sell the Indians liquor that most of them spend all in drunkenness.*

In an ill-fated frenzy to protect the remains of his ancestors' domain from the Englishmen's further encroachment, Philip in the summer of 1675 rallied tribes up and down the Hudson to join in a summer war dance, and thence move out to attack English settlements. Casualties of King Philip's War numbered 200 colonial militia and 1,000 Indians, including Philip. Hundreds of Indian captives, including many who had been promised protection on surrender, were sold into slavery in the West Indies. Despite the pleading of John Eliot, Philip's wife and nine-year-old son were sold into slavery to Bermuda. Philip's head rotted on a pike high on a hill overlooking Plymouth Colony, over which today a statue of Massasoit imposingly stands. Generations of American school children in less-than-authentic Indian costumes have commemorated Thanksgiving, fleetingly noting the role of Massasoit, but not remembering his grandson, who a scant half century after that first Thanksgiving died in an effort to save his ancestors' domain.

Before and after the King Philip episode, the rigid New Englanders promoted a theory, spoken and written, which equated native peoples with forces of evil — children-of-darkness, children-of-Satan. This theory was used with artful cunning to justify dispossession of Native peoples of their lands and cultures. Smallpox, a European import, became "the evident hand of Heaven. . .extinguishing whole nations of the savage" to prove God intended America for the English. Cotton Mather described Indians as "doleful creatures. . .the veriest ruines of mankind. . .abominable, slothful and perfidious wretches."

The church in New England left another legacy with which 20th century stewardship committees must yet deal. The climate of dependency of Christian

Indians can be traced to 17th century Massachusetts legal documents. In 1644 measures were adopted for "civilizing and evangelizing" and ministers were designated to instruct Indians. Provisions were made for "gifts for Indians willing to receive instructions."

While John Eliot is credited, by Cotton Mather, with "blessed labor which bore much fruit" in his 46 years of mission and ministry among American Indians, the most consequential of Eliot's achievements was his role in establishing the first and oldest missionary society of the Anglican Church. Of more importance perhaps, than his getting the first Bibles printed in America was Eliot's getting his tracts published in England. These tracts cemented the foundation of the Society for Propagation of the Gospel in Foreign Parts (SPG). Initiated in the reign of Charles I, supported by Cromwell (under whose direction 12,000 pounds were raised in England and Wales), SPG was reinforced by Charles II and became a major tool of Queen Anne at the dawn of the 18th century in bringing the gospel to American Indians. From the coffers of SPG, until the outbreak of the American Revolution, came the wherewithal to fund the Jamestown commitment which specified:

> . . .the true word of God be preached, planted and used not only in the colonies, but also as much as might be, among the savages bordering upon them, and this according to the rites and doctrines of the Church of England.

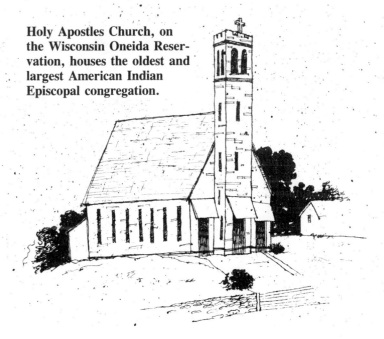

Holy Apostles Church, on the Wisconsin Oneida Reservation, houses the oldest and largest American Indian Episcopal congregation.

**Rising Sun, the persistent Chippewa of
Turtle Mountain, and his wife**

Chapter 4

The Anglican/Episcopal Church and the great Iroquois Confederacy

Today in the rolling green hills of eastern Wisconsin there thrives the largest American Indian congregation of the Episcopal Church. Listing 2,000 baptized and 900 communicants, Holy Apostles on the Oneida Reservation is also the oldest Native American congregation, tracing its grounding to the reign of Queen Anne, when the Oneida lived in their traditional homeland in central New York state. In 1703 the Oneida requested English missionaries from Queen Anne, and in 1816, the Episcopal Church began its mother mission to American Indians among the Oneida. Woven into the colorful history of Holy Apostles are stalwart tribal leaders, zealous Anglican missionaries, patriots of the American Revolution, and a man who claimed to be the lost dauphin of France.

The Oneida were a member nation of the six-nation Iroquois Confederacy, which several centuries before white contact had established a representative form of government under the Great Law of Peace. Other member nations were the Mohawk, Onondaga, Cayuga and Seneca, and early in the 18th century the Tuscarora of North Carolina joined as the sixth nation of the league. Each nation retained its identity, but the union was strong. In the first English account of the Iroquois league, Cadwallader Colden in 1727 wrote in his *History of the Five Indian Nations Depending on the Province of New York in America,* stating:

> *The five nations [are] joyn'd together by a League or Confederacy. . . without any Superiority of any one over the other. This Union has continued so long that the Christians know nothing of the Original of it.*

The Iroquois (Haudenosaunee) people have a traditional story about the formation of their confederacy and the law that governed it. In a special issue on Indian contributions to the U. S. Constitution, Cindy Darcy, in Friends Committee on National Legislation's *Washington Newsletter,* August-September, 1987, retold the story:

> *A very long time ago, in a time of blood feuding, intertribal warfare, and terror, the Peacemaker went first to the Mohawks and then to the other four nations, offering the idea that all human beings possessed the power of rational thought. Rational thought enabled people to negotiate with others and create the conditions for peace.*

Peace between nations was to be not only the absence of violence, but also the active presence of creative interactions which would build a better, more whole world in the future. Peacemaker took his message from village to village and nation to nation throughout the lands of the Haudenosaunee. The first person to accept Peacemaker's message was the "Peace Mother." Eventually, all five nations agreed to Peacemaker's vision of peace, and gathered in council at Onondaga, in the center of the Nations, to set down the principles of the Gayaneshakgowa or the Great Law of Peace.

The Great Law of Peace established laws and a code of conduct for the Iroquois nations. The 117-section Great Law was first written down in the 19th century, recorded previously on wampum belts, and passed from generation to generation by oral tradition, as it is today.

The Great Law of Peace contains many of the principles found in American government today, including the recognition of the rights to freedom of speech and religion, the right of women to participate in the government, separation of powers, and checks and balances between branches of governments.

As the flame for the American Revolution was kindled, Benjamin Franklin looked to the Iroquois Confederacy for a model to form a union which would provide both individual freedom and corporate strength. The framers of the American nation borrowed the Iroquois model as the political structure of the United States; yet, it was the War of the American Revolution which broke forever the power of the great Iroquois Confederacy.

Out of New York state have flowed policies and practices of crown and colonies — and later church and state — which shaped concept and law relating to interaction of Indians and the whites and which continue in force today. The concept of sovereignty of Indian nations — still esteemed paramount in the late 20th century by some 300 Indian nations — was grounded in the system of interchange through treaties which gave Europeans control over Indians' land but, lastingly, established acceptance by Europeans of nationhood of Indian groups. What is said to be the first treaty ever made between Europeans and Indians was negotiated in New York between Jacob Elkins and the Iroquois.

Dutch settlers were the first Europeans to arrive in New York. In 1626, so goes the story, Peter Minuet bought Manhattan Island from a group of Indians for trinkets worth 60 guilders, then equivalent to about $24. In Manhattan real estate, however, nothing is simple, and it is said that the Indians with whom Minuet was dealing were only passing through, and that the Dutch had to repurchase the island a few years later at an undisclosed price from the rightful residents. So it is said.

While the Dutch Reformed pastors had contact with the Iroquois and translated the Bible, the Dutch West Indies Company was primarily business motivated. Records indicate, however, that the Dutch treated Indians fairly and kept promises made.

In 1664 the English took New Amsterdam and named it New York. With the English settlers came the English church. Trinity Church was organized in 1696, and one of Trinity's rectors is credited with translating and publishing a Book of Common Prayer for the Mohawks. Some half-hearted efforts were made in the early 1700s to send missionaries to the Iroquois in part, no doubt at first, to detach them from French interests. The Roman Catholic Church was brought by the French, and by the mid-1600s there were missions among all five Iroquois nations with 2,000 converts, the best known being Kateri Tekakwitha, the Lily of the Mohawks, the first American Indian candidate for canonization by the Roman church.

In 1704 the Church of England sent the Mohawks the Rev. Thoroughgood Moore, the first missionary to the Indians funded by the SPG. The SPG funding for mission among Indians was niggardly and sporadic, and within a year Moore had departed. In 1710 a group of Iroquois chiefs was taken to London and had an audience with Queen Anne. Among them was the Mohawk Sagayeathquapiethtow, said to have been grandfather of Thayendanegea, who would be known as Joseph Brant and figure prominently in politics of church and state before the end of the century. The chiefs were presented in formal ceremony at St. James Palace where, on cue, they expressed distrust of the French, against whom they were preparing war, and reminded the queen of an earlier promise to send them military assistance. Through their interpreter they also conveyed:

> *Since we were in Covenant with our Great Queen's Children, we have had some knowledge of the Saviour of the World, and have often been opportuned by the French Priests and Presents, but ever esteemed them as men of Falsehood, but if our Great Queen would send some to Instruct us, they should find a most hearty Welcome.*

Mindful of potential for French encroachment on her New York colony, the Queen made haste to help her children of the Iroquois Confederacy. Her first mission work was principally among the Mohawk, the eastern-most nation of the league, and by 1712 the first chapel for the Mohawks was built at Fort Hunter on the Mohawk River. Toward furnishing the Mohawk chapel, the queen sent altar plate and linen. The Archbishop of Canterbury sent 12 large Bibles and a table. Though the SPG cut off funds within five years, the mission survived. Then, in 1743, the Rev. Henry Barclay was "sent out," and small Anglican chapels soon appeared all along the banks of the Mohawk River, which meanders eastward through the slopes of central New York to the Hudson. Within six years Barclay reported that only a few of the Mohawk remained unbaptized.

Shortly thereafter came Sir William Johnson, the crown's Indian commissioner, who with the powerful Mohawk leader, Captain Joseph Brant, cemented a solid bond between the Mohawk and the British crown and Church of England which would survive the American Revolution.

Joseph Brant: loyalist

Likely the best known American Indian of the 18th century, Joseph Brant lived and died loyal to the crown and the Church of England. He was a younger brother of the bright and capricious Molly Brant, loyal consort of Sir William Johnson, Indian commissioner from 1746 until his death in 1774. Brant was baptized at the Mohawk town of Canajoharie where the English church maintained a church and school. He was further educated by the English at the Connecticut school of the Rev. Eleazar Wheelock, who would later found Dartmouth College. While at the Wheelock school, Brant instructed a young Puritan minister who was having difficulty in mastering the Mohawk language. He was Samuel Kirkland who was to labor 40 years among the Iroquois, primarily the Oneida.

Sir William, who influenced the confederacy to fight with the British in their protracted clashes with the French along their colonial borders, died on the eve of the American Revolution. When the war came, the British again sought the assistance of the Iroquois; the Continental Congress sought their neutrality. When the question came to the council of the league, decision was ultimately left to each nation, and only the Oneida declared for neutrality. As the war went on, Samuel Kirkland eventually delivered the Oneida and Tuscaroras to the side of the colonists; the Mohawk, Onondaga, Cayuga and Seneca all eventually took up the King's cause.

July of 1776 found Captain Brant returning from England. Upon reaching New York City, held during the Revolution by the British, he volunteered his services to General Howe and the loyalists. In the late summer of 1776, Brant distinguished himself in the Battle of Long Island as a soldier and strategist. Subsequently, the British command granted his request to slip through the American lines in disguise to return to the Iroquois where he was given a hero's welcome. Brant rallied warriors of the Iroquois to take up the cause of the King and in doing so he split the confederacy and uprooted the Great Tree of Peace.

In 1779 the colonial army swept westward to destroy the loyalist Iroquois stronghold, burning towns and corn fields. In the inventory of items "liberated" by the colonial army were the fancy ball gowns of Molly Brant, the Mohawk matron.

After the peace treaty between Great Britain and the United States in 1783,

Brant received a tract of land on the Grand River in Ontario, 60 miles west of Niagara Falls, on which he settled pro-British Mohawk and other Iroquois followers. After all the years of toil of the Anglican Church among the "Keepers of the Eastern Door," the Mohawk, all that remains of the first major Anglican/Episcopal mission is an abandoned cemetery on the St. Regis-Akwesasne Reservation at the northern tip of the state of New York.

Described by his old teacher, Eleazar Wheelock, as a man of "sprightly genius," Brant was forerunner of generations of Native peoples who would be caught inextricably in the clash between white and Indian cultures. He had been born and educated in traditional Mohawk ways, but he had also received an education from the English missionaries. While he was equipped to walk in both worlds, he was never really accepted — except as a curiosity — in the white world, nor was he any longer, in an unqualified sense, a Mohawk.

During the last 25 years of his life, Brant resided in baronial graciousness on the Grand River (or Six Nations) Reserve in Canada. There he translated the Anglican Book of Common Prayer and the Gospel of St. Mark. On the reserve a chapel was built — identified today as the first protestant chapel in the province of Ontario — and on its grounds Brant was buried. To the Chapel of St. Paul, in 1788, a former missionary at Canajoharie delivered part of the communion silver which had been the gift of Queen Anne to "her Mohawk children."

Queen Anne sent a second set of silver. To the Onondaga she sent a chalice, two flagons and three patens with the following inscription:

The Gift of Her Majesty
Anne
By Grace of God
Queen
of Great Britain, France and Ireland, and
all her Plantations in North America
to her Indian Chappell on the Onondaga.

The gift of the gracious queen to her Indian chapel on the Onondaga was untimely; the chapel did not then exist. The queen's silver reposes, yet, at St. Peter's Church in Albany.

Church of the Good Shepherd on the Onondaga

The present-day Episcopal mission on the Onondaga Reservation, the Church of the Good Shepherd, has sought on occasion to reclaim the gift of Queen Anne to the people of the Onondaga.

The church, with 150 communicants, is one of but two predominantly-Indian Episcopal congregations in the state of New York where early Anglican influence was strongest and in which reside, according to 1980 Census,

39,000 American Indians. Five of the six nations of the Iroquois still have small reservations with functioning tribal governments and services. Only the Cayuga are landless. In recent decades, which saw unprecedented resurgence of Indian assertion of a proud heritage, new friction arose between some Indians of the Iroquois nations who are Christian and those who practice the traditional longhouse religion. Tension is more visible on the Onondaga Reservation, which strongly asserts its sovereignty and has issued its own passports.

The Onondaga congregation has existed since 1868. The white frame Church of the Good Shepherd was consecrated in 1870 by the Rt. Rev. Frederick Dan Huntington, the first bishop of Central New York. Old newspaper clippings indicate a good relationship between the people of the longhouse religion and the Christian community at that time; one article notes that ". . .a leading Indian Chief, Captain George, was present during the entire consecration ceremony. . ."

Widows of priests were vital to continuity of the mission and lived on the reservation to serve the congregation. Mrs. William Manross, resident from 1919 until 1937, started the first health clinic for children; Mrs. Charles Harris Jr., resident from 1941-1952, raised funds to build a mission hall, still used for reservation community services. Work of these two women was highly respected among the matrilineal Onondaga.

Church of the Good Shepherd on the Seneca Cattaraugus Reservation

During the summer of 1986 an informal companion relationship was renewed between the Onondaga congregation and New York state's only other American Indian Episcopal congregation, located 180 miles away. Good Shepherd on the Seneca Cattaraugus Reservation at Irving in the Diocese of Western New York lists 100 baptized communicants. It was founded in 1901. The two congregations have articulated their sense of isolation from the church's growing Indian ministry in the west, and their respective vestries and priests-in-charge have recently renewed their ties, meeting to share mutual concerns. In 1987 the two congregations designated a joint representative to the National Committee on Indian Work.

The Seneca, "Keepers of the Western Door," had largely resisted the considerable early missionizing efforts of both the French Jesuits and Anglicans. Even Samuel Kirkland, the Puritan, who exercised great influence with the Oneida, made little headway in either evangelizing the Seneca or convincing them to fight the British. Kirkland, educated at Wheelock's innovative school, was an ardent patriot and had an official relationship with the Continental Congress which earned him commendation from General Washington.

Traditional lands of the Seneca encompassed much of western New York and from the 1600s through the Revolution they were victims of the power struggle between nations of Europe. During the Revolution, the Seneca to a certain extent joined the Mohawks in loyalty to Britain, and as a result sustained awful punishment by the colonial army, which marched out with orders not only to overrun but destroy. General John Sullivan razed 40 villages and burned 160,000 bushels of corn, leveled orchard after orchard and field upon field. Iroquois power never recovered. But out of the demoralization came a hope for the future advanced by the Seneca prophet, Handsome Lake, who brought vision of a new religion, a faith which combined certain Quaker religious tenets and traditional Iroquois ways. The Code of Handsome Lake was quickly accepted, not only by the Senecas, but by others of the old Iroquois Confederacy.

The Revolution, of course, devastated American Indian missions of the Church of England. Anglican activity ceased; financial support to mission programs from the SPG was no more. Almost half a century would pass before any work among Indians was begun under the banner of the new Episcopal Church.

Williams: the lost dauphin of France, or St. Regis Mohawk?

Grandfather to American Indian Episcopal mission was John Henry Hobart, bishop of New York. His grandson, William Hobart Hare, a half century later, would become shepherd to the great Sioux nation of the northern plains as bishop of Niobrara. The elder established the first Episcopal Indian mission; the grandson established more than 90 new Sioux missions.

Bishop Hobart, consecrated in 1811, was keenly conscious of Anglican heritage among the Iroquois nations. He looked at the Oneida, residing to the east of the Finger Lakes region, as the people among whom to initiate his work, and within four years of his consecration, he had begun the first Episcopal Indian mission. It would be the only one for the next 37 years.

A key figure in stabilizing the Oneida mission was a man of much mystery. He was Eleazar Williams, whose origins have been argued interminably. Some believed him to be Louis XVII, the lost dauphin of France, son of Louis XVI and Marie Antoinette, brought to America as a child to escape death in the French Revolution. Others theorized he was descendant of the Rev. John Williams of Massachusetts, whose family had been captured by Indians in 1704 and taken to Canada. There was a legend that the Williams daughter, Eunice, had a son fathered by a St. Regis Mohawk. It was from the St. Regis Reservation that Eleazar Williams first appeared. He attended school in New England, returned to St. Regis to teach Mohawks for the Roman Catholics, and after involvement in the War of 1812 appeared on the Oneida Reservation.

Williams was received with kindness among the Oneida, and on observing that Christian teachers had already worked among the Oneida, he sought an interview with Bishop Hobart. The bishop was impressed with Williams' plan to bring the tribe into the Episcopal Church and commissioned him as catechist and lay reader. Williams rearranged Brant's Mohawk prayer book, and with help of Bishop Hobart had it published. Within three years the Oneida nation had moved toward broad acceptance of the Episcopal Church, and Williams became a postulant for the diaconate.

Because he failed to clarify his origins — historians sense he actually believed himself to be the lost dauphin — he cannot be identified as the first American Indian ordained by the Episcopal Church. His influence in secular affairs of the Oneida was pivotal; he encouraged the treaty that sent the Oneida westward. Additionally, there has remained a question on how deeply Williams was involved with the Ogden Company which surreptitiously grabbed title to most of the land of the nations of the Iroquois.

A little church, built by the Oneida themselves, was consecrated in 1819 under the name of St. Peter's. On that occasion, Bishop Hobart confirmed 56 persons and baptized two adults and 46 infants. The Oneidas had not long to enjoy their little church building. The early 1800s brought the forced migration of eastern Indians, a heartless effort spurred relentlessly by Andrew Jackson. A fraudulent treaty was ratified by the Senate which would have dispersed all the nations of the proud and once powerful Iroquois Confederacy. However, through intervention by the Quakers, Jackson to some extent relented. Some Seneca and Cayuga along with a few Mohawk were eventually dispatched to Oklahoma, and the Oneida were removed to Wisconsin.

Many of the Oneida were opposed to removal. Williams encouraged the removal, extolling prospects of new hope in the west. In 1822 the Oneida acquired from the Menominee Tribe a 100-square-mile reservation located at Duck Creek, 10 miles west of Green Bay, Wisconsin. In 1823 Williams accompanied Chief Skenandoah and the Oneidas to their new home.

At first, each Sunday the Oneida gathered to worship beneath the trees on Duck Creek. Then, in 1825, the first church building in Wisconsin was erected. By special permission, the Oneida named their church for their "father" back in New York, Bishop Hobart. The New York bishop visited the small hand-hewn log Hobart Church, and in 1838, the Oneida hosted the Rt. Rev. Jackson Kemper, the first missionary bishop of the Episcopal Church. Bishop Kemper laid the cornerstone for a new frame church which would replace the old log structure.

Cornelius Hill: first Oneida priest

William Adams and James Lloyd Breck, founders of Nashotah House seminary, walked more than a hundred miles through pathless forests to Hobart Church to be ordained. It was the only consecrated building in Wisconsin. As a memorial of their ordination, the Oneida people gave the two young clergymen a bell, which was later known at Nashotah House as "old Michael."

The Nashotah founders took back with them a promising 12-year-old Oneida, Cornelius Hill, who was to become the youngest chief and first Oneida priest. A staunch supporter of the missionaries throughout his life, Chief Hill also led his people in a successful opposition to a further move west: ". . .you seek to drive us from our lands again — NO!"

He served as interpreter and organist in the Oneida church through many years and on June 27, 1885, he was ordained deacon. For reasons unexplained, it was not until 1903 that the Indian was ordained priest. Two hundred guests and the Oneida brass band appeared for ordination day, both a happy and sad day; Hill's son, who died of whooping cough, was buried on the same day. Hill died in 1907, only four years after his priesting, and is buried in Holy Apostles churchyard.

Today there stands on the Oneida Wisconsin Reservation a handsome stone church building which was begun in 1870 and rebuilt after a 1920 fire. Stone for the building was quarried from the reservation and Oneida men each week gave one day's wages toward its building fund. Women and children picked berries to be sold in the neighboring towns, and women made and sold handicrafts to contribute to the building fund. After 14 years, $6,000 had been raised, but the Green Bay bank, where the money was deposited, failed and all was lost. An appeal throughout the diocese netted $5,000 and work was continued. Finally, in 1886, the cornerstone of the new church was laid by John Henry Hobart Brown, the first bishop of the Diocese of Fond du Lac, and a member of the family of Bishop Hobart of New York.

The present bishop of Fond du Lac, William Louis Stevens, came to Holy Apostles on July 26, 1986, for solemn ceremonies to celebrate the 100th anniversary of laying the cornerstone and to open a year-long series of special events to celebrate Holy Apostles' life among the Oneida people. Gone are the hospital, the school and the convent of the Sisters of the Holy Nativity, but a solid Anglo-catholic congregation of Oneida Christians had continued, except for the American Revolution interruption, since the reign of Queen Anne.

William S. Cross, first North Dakota
Indian ordained priest

Chapter 5

Episcopal mission in the Great Lakes area and northern plains

Until 1852 the Episcopal Church maintained only one mission among American Indians. Within the next decade, however, spirited new mission work began in the Great Lakes area and spread to the northern plains where it has continued uninterrupted for 135 years. Two men, in wholly different style, were most responsible for guiding the Episcopal Church to honor the Jamestown commitment. They were Bishop Henry Benjamin Whipple of Minnesota and Bishop William Hobart Hare of Niobrara.

The bishops arrived to assume oversight of their respective jurisdictions at a critical hour in Indian-white relations. The federal government's Office of Indian Affairs was abysmally corrupt; the doctrine of manifest destiny was poised for its last and final thrust; the lakes and woodlands tribes were barely subsisting in unbelievable conditions, while the plains peoples were engaged in a last desperate resistance to the white conquerors.

While hesitant mission had been started in 1852 in northern Minnesota, its continuity was insured in 1859 when there burst onto the Episcopal scene one of the most dynamic and picturesque men ever to sit in the House of Bishops, Henry Benjamin Whipple, first bishop of Minnesota. Only 37 when be became bishop, the native New Yorker would head the Minnesota diocese for 42 years. Almost single-handedly, Whipple awakened in the Episcopal Church a social consciousness about Indian affairs and conducted last rites for the church's appalling apathy.

Fourteen years later, in 1873, another key player, of entirely different temperament, stepped on stage. Literally hand-picked by Whipple, William Hobart Hare established the Episcopal Church among the Lakota/Dakota tribes, confirming 10,000 in the great Sioux nation, coming as a bishop for the non-geographic Missionary Jurisdiction of Niobrara, which a decade later became the Missionary District of South Dakota.

Aroused primarily by these two stalwarts, the Episcopal mission among American Indians over the next century was essentially centered in the region of the Great Lakes and northern plains, today's dioceses of Minnesota, North and South Dakota. It was there that the Episcopal Church ordained the first American Indian to the priesthood, and 113 years later consecrated its first American Indian to the episcopate.

It was there that the first Episcopal Indian boarding schools were built, albeit hand-in-glove with the federal government, which had as its goal wholesale annihilation of Indian languages, cultures and identity. Nonetheless, it was in Minnesota and subsequently the Dakotas that the Episcopal Church got serious about American Indian mission and ministry, and as a result, approximately one-half of today's Episcopal Native Americans trace their affiliation with the church to early ministry of the north woods and prairies.

Whipple and Hare cast imperatives that would affect the Episcopal Church for generations. Ever the extrovert, Whipple wandered the world; he is glimpsed in Cairo, Alaska, Palestine, Cambridge and Constantinople. He had audiences with the mighty — the President of the United States, the Archbishop of Canterbury, and Queen Victoria. Hare also traveled — some of the Indians called him Swift Bird — but his journeys were to crisscross his vast jurisdiction establishing missions and chapels, schools and substations.

Both bishops had association with treaty commissions of the tumultuous times. Hare declined appointment to a commission in late 1876 to "negotiate sale of the Black Hills." However, he sanctioned commission participation of two of his priests, Samuel Hinman and Edward Ashley. The former almost immediately fell into disfavor with the bishop and was driven away; the latter would serve as a priest in South Dakota for 57 years and bear the title of archdeacon of Niobrara. An article in *The Church at Work,* October 1923, informs that Ashley was then the "sole white survivor of the group which framed the agreement of 1876 that opened the Black Hills to white settlement." Whipple's autobiography reveals that he, too, in the immediate aftermath of the Sioux victory at the battle of Little Bighorn, traveled 200 miles by wagon with a treaty commission which met with the Sioux Chief Spotted Tail. Whipple described Spotted Tail as a "picture of manly beauty, with piercing eyes, self-possessed," and quoted the Brule as saying:

> ...*The white man wants another treaty? Why does not the Great Father put his red children on wheels, so that he can move them as he will?*

That Whipple advocated the reservation system is known; the extent to which he influenced the congressional action in 1877 that illegally took the Black Hills from the Sioux nations is not known.

The two bishops came to Indian nations which were historic enemies and spoke different languages. Frequent skirmishes occurred between the Lakota/Dakota (Sioux) plains people, to whom Hare was sent, and the Ojibwas (Chippewa) of the north woods, to whom Whipple first ministered. Among the legends on derivation of the word "Sioux," is a story that early French explorers asked their Ojibwa guides about the people who wore great feathered headdress and rode fast ponies, and through the popular press of the late 19th century would become imprinted on the minds of the dominant society as prototype for all American Indians. The Ojibwa described the Dakota as "Na-do-wes-sue," a word which translated as enemy or snake in the Ojibwa language. "Ah," concluded the Frenchmen, "these people are Sioux," adopting the French spelling. The United States government, in its tangled and often embittered relations with the many Lakota/Dakota bands, who spoke different but related languages, identified them as Sioux. So did the church. There is also a story on how the Ojibwa came to be called Chippewa. The word is a misbegotten pronunciation of a denigrating Dakota word meaning "people of the puckered moccasins." Many Ojibwa people today prefer to be called Anishinaabe, meaning in their own language, simply, "the people."

Whipple and Hare were keys to bringing the gospel of Jesus Christ to the people of the plains and north woods. Lamentable is the fact that the good news was brought westward fashioned from the early New England missionizing blueprint, rife with paternalism and enshrouded in ethnocentrism. A Lakota priest recently mused on early inflexible missionary dictates. He said, "If only the church had just brought us the gospel of Jesus and offered it to us as fulfillment and supplement to our own native traditional spirituality without demanding that we disclaim all our inherent values. We were deeply spiritual people with reverence for all creation, and our spirituality permeated every aspect of our lives. The church, however, required us to disavow all our old values. We men were even required to cut our braids before baptism. I sometimes wonder how well St. Paul would have fared when he introduced the gospel to Europe if he had instituted a dress code on the Macedonians."

Enmegahbowh: first American Indian ordained to priesthood

Church historians have slighted the role of an Indian man, Enmegahbowh, in chronicling the coming of Christianity to the Ojibwa of northern Minnesota. While Whipple was the broker, Enmegahbowh was the implementer. While Whipple would come to be known as Apostle to the Indians, it was Enmegahbowh who served as the bishop's enabler, loyal companion, associate, and interpreter for more than 40 years.

It was Enmegahbowh, in fact, who first invited Episcopal mission among the Indians of Minnesota. Born in Canada around 1813 and a member of the Ottawa tribe, Enmegahbowh — his name means One-who-stands-before-his-people — was living in an Ottawa encampment near the village of Peterborough, Ontario, when he first came to the notice of an Anglican clergyman. The minister, identified only as Mr. Armour, persuaded Enmegahbowh's reluctant parents to allow the young boy to live in his home to be educated with his sons. After three months, when Enmegahbowh had learned to read and to speak English, homesickness drove him to run away in the night and travel on foot for two days to reach his people.

Sketchy accounts next provide a glimpse of Enmegahbowh in northern Minnesota where he had been ordained deacon under the name of John Johnson by the Methodists. They expelled him from their ranks following an incident in 1849. It is said that a white man insulted Enmegahbowh's wife Charlotte and that Enmegahbowh knocked the man down and held him while his wife gave the worthless man a sound beating.

Following the incident, Enmegahbowh came into contact with an Episcopal chaplain serving with the U. S. Army at Fort Snelling, Minnesota. The chaplain told Enmegahbowh of the work in Wisconsin of Dr. James Lloyd Breck, who in 1851 left Nashotah House and started a mission at St. Paul. Enmegahbowh, who apparently had joined a band of Chippewas on Gull Lake, located around 150 miles to the northwest, came to St. Paul and left his son to be educated at the mission. Later Enmegahbowh sent an appeal to the Breck: "Come you, Come and teach."

The mother mission of Indian work west of the Mississippi

Breck responded, joining Enmegahbowh in 1852, at Gull Lake, named in Ojibwa Ka-ge-ash-koon-si-kag, "the place of the little gulls." Together, they established St. Columba's, the mother mission of Episcopal Indian work west of the Mississippi River.

Breck soon departed the Ojibwa mission to found Seabury Divinity School in Faribault, Minnesota, and Enmegahbowh remained at Gull Lake. He was substantially assisted by missionaries of the Church of England working in Canada, who shared an Ojibwa translation of the prayer book, the four gospels and later the complete New Testament.

On May 5, 1854, Enmegahbowh formally applied to be admitted as candidate for Holy Orders. Jackson Kemper, the legendary missionary bishop of the vast west, accepted him and on July 3, 1859, as one of his last acts as the provisional bishop of the diocese, Kemper ordained Enmegahbowh to the diaconate. Eight years later Enmegahbowh was ordained to the priesthood.

On October 13, 1859, Whipple was consecrated bishop of Minnesota and during the lights and shadows of his long episcopate he became known far and wide as the champion of Indians in their dealings with the government of the United States, as well as their chief pastor and friend. A scant month following his consecration, Whipple set out with Breck to visit Enmegahbowh at the Gull Lake Mission. The bishop wrote of his first visit:

> No words can describe the pitiable condition of these Indians. A few miles from St. Columba we came to a wigwam where the half-naked children were crying from cold and hunger, and the mother was scraping the inner bark of the pine tree for pitch to give to her starving children...

> Our Indian affairs are at their worst; without government, without protection, without personal rights of property, subject to every evil influence, and the prey of covetous, dishonest white men, while the fire-water flowed in rivers of death...

In 1867, 73 years after the consecration of Samuel Seabury as the first bishop of the American church, Whipple ordained the first American Indian to the priesthood. For eight years Enmegahbowh had been a deacon serving under various white missionaries at Gull Lake, but when one more Gull Lake white missionary departed to become an army chaplain, Enmegahbowh was again left in charge of the growing mission. Whipple acted:

> *It was one hundred miles to the nearest priest, and the Holy Communion could be administered only at my visits. Enmegahbowh had a good English education, was devout, and well-read in the scriptures and in Church history.*
>
> *With consent of the Standing Committee, I gave him a dispensation for the Greek and Hebrew. . . My Indian did not miss an answer in his examinations by three of the ablest men in my diocese. I ordained Enmegahbowh to the priesthood in the Cathedral at Faribault, and I knew my red children could henceforth receive the Christian bread.*

First mission among the Dakota: ill-fated Santee Sioux

In the second year of his episcopacy, Whipple visited the Lower Sioux Agency of the Santee band of Dakotas at Redwood, Minnesota, and heard a plea for a missionary and a school. The bishop sent the Rev. Samuel Dutton Hinman along with his young bride to establish the Santee Mission. The work at Redwood ended in tragedy on August 18, 1862, in the early hours of the Dakota Conflict.

By 1862 the Santee Sioux had lost all their land except a strip 10 miles wide and 150 miles long along the south side of the Minnesota River. In payment for their many land cessions, the Santee were to receive annuities in goods, food and cash. They were flagrantly exploited and cheated by white traders. In 1862 their annuity payment was delayed, and delayed again. July passed — the time for their annual buffalo hunt — and still they huddled around the agency awaiting the treaty-obligated annuity. Wise men knew confrontation was inevitable. The land was gone, the buffalo was going and the treaty-guaranteed food supply failed to arrive.

The "uprising" was triggered by a trivial incident. Twenty young men, returning from an unsuccessful hunt, passed near a white settlement and found a nest of eggs. What began as a dare among angry young men on a Sunday afternoon to steal eggs ended with a challenge to test manhood. Before sundown five white settlers were dead. Through the night the Santee chiefs argued. Wabasha, a Christian, argued for peace. He lost. Before the summer was over 700 white settlers and 100 Indians were killed in the tragic conflict.

The distinguished award-winning Sioux author, Virginia Driving Hawk Sneve, daughter of an Episcopal priest, has written a comprehensive history of the Episcopal mission among her people, *That They May Have Life: The Episcopal Church in South Dakota 1859 - 1976.* She has given permission to quote liberally from her work on both the Santee tragedy and subsequent sketches on the Diocese of South Dakota:

> *The [Episcopal] work at Redwood ended on August 18, 1862. The Sioux broke out of the narrow confines of their Minnesota Valley reservation in a desperate, doomed uprising against long years of government treachery and deceit. Many of the Christian Santee saved white missionaries and settlers, but all were considered equally guilty of the white settlers' deaths and were imprisoned at Fort Snelling. The Rev. Hinman accompanied the Santee to the fort to give what comfort he could in the face of the angry white residents of Minnesota who were demanding extermination of the "merciless" savages or, barring that, their complete removal from Minnesota.*
>
> *The Rev. Hinman and the Presbyterian missionaries who ministered to the Santee were victims of the vindictiveness of the white population. Hinman was beaten unconscious by a band of toughs who broke into the stockade. He and others defending the Indians were called avaricious priests and denounced as mawkish sentimentalists and contemptible fools.*
>
> *The Santee, in the misery of their destitution, turned to the missionaries for aid. Many now realized the need for strong faith in their lives in this time of distress and accepted the Christian God.*
>
> *The Rev. Hinman lived at the fort, opened a school, baptized 149, and had as many as 300 Indians under his care. When Bishop Whipple visited the prison, he confirmed 100 Santee.*
>
> *On February 16, 1863, the United States government abrogated all treaties with the Santee Sioux, and gave their annuity payments to white families of those who were killed. Minnesota never wanted a Sioux Indian within its borders again.*
>
> *The Santee were assigned a new reservation in Dakota Territory, near Crow Creek on the Missouri River, and a stockade was built which enclosed the agency buildings and barracks. The journey to their new home began at Fort Snelling, where the Indians were herded onto steamers and shipped down the Mississippi like cattle, crowded into a small craft which forced them to sleep in shifts because there was not enough room for all to lie down. The conditions were insufferable and the food bad, as they moved up the Missouri River to their new home.*

It was Enmegahbowh who influenced the Ojibwa not to join the Dakota in the clash. There were frequent accounts of lives of whites being saved by

Christian Sioux. Cited specifically were Episcopal converts: Chief Wabasha, Taopi, Good Thunder, Iron Shield, Simon A-Nag-mani, Lorenzo, Laurence, Other Day, Thomas Robertson, Wakin-yo-ta-wa and Paul Mazakute, who would become, in 1868, the first full-blooded Sioux ordained to the diaconate in the Episcopal Church.

Swift vengeance of the whites followed the conflicts. Two thousand Indians, the Christian peace group as well as the hostiles, were rounded up. Four hundred suspects were identified in a process that lasted about five minutes each. "Trials" ended with 306 death sentences. Whipple intervened directly with President Lincoln, who commuted death sentences for all but 38. At Mankato on the day after Christmas, 1862, one rope on a specially constructed scaffold was cut and 38 condemned Dakotas were hanged. There was at least one case of mistaken identity. As the condemned 38 walked to their execution, it is said they sang the Dakota Chant memorialized in today's Episcopal Hymnal (hymn 385).

Bishop Whipple awakens the church to Indian advocacy

Whipple went to the Episcopal General Convention of 1862 and for the first of many times, stirred his brother bishops into visible advocacy around Indian issues:

> *I went to General Convention sick at heart, and the more depressed because I was half ill from having poisoned my hand severely in caring for the wounds of the sufferers. . .I drew up a paper [see appendix X] to present to the President of the United States and showed it to one of the bishops, who after reading it said, "I hope you will not bring politics into the House."*
>
> *Bishop Alonzo Potter (Pennsylvania), observing my distress, asked me the cause, and I answered, "My diocese is desolated by Indian war; eight hundred of our people are dead, and I have just come from a hospital of dead and dying. I asked one of my brothers to sign this paper and he responds by calling it 'politics.'" In his own warm-hearted way the bishop exclaimed, "My dear Minnesota, give me the paper. I will get it signed, and will go to Washington with Bishop McIlvvaine (Ohio) and present it."*

Whipple in his autobiography provides a fleeting glimpse of Enmegah-bowh at the beginning of the Sioux uprising. In *Lights and Shadows of a Long Episcopate,* the bishop wrote that when Enmegahbowh got word of the Sioux plan to attack he had

> *. . .walked all night down the Gull River, dragging a canoe containing his wife and children, that he might give warning to the fort. Two of his children died from exposure. . .*

45

No white person rallied to warn Indians in an earlier incident related by Enmegahbowh and included in the Whipple autobiography. Indians from all the Mississippi lands — Mille Lacs, Gull Lake, Leech Lake and Pokeguma — had assembled for government rations. Enmegahbowh wrote his bishop:

> *The old Sandy Point was covered with wigwams. The first day they received their beautiful well-colored flour hard with lumps, the pork heavily perfumed. The old chief brought me some of both and said, "Is this fit to eat?" I said, "No, it is not fit to eat."*
>
> *But the Indians were hungry and they ate it. About ten o'clock, the first gun was fired. You well know, Bishop, that Indians fire a gun when a death occurs. An hour after another gun was fired, then another and another, until it seemed death was at every wigwam. That night, twenty children died, and the next day as many more, and so for five days and five nights, the deaths went on.*
>
> *Bishop, when these dear victims strewed along the pathless wilderness shall hear the great trumpet sound and shall point to those who caused their death, it will be dreadful!*
>
> *My friend, Chief Pakanuhwaush, has just come in. I asked him how many died at the payment at Sandy Lake. He said, "Over three hundred."*

Rotten meat, dishonest Indian agents, deliberate deception — all these unconscionable practices were rampant across the Indian country to which Whipple came. The bishop, a tall ruddy-faced man with a determined chin and generous mouth, took on the challenge of reform of the U.S. government's Indian policy, carrying the cause of Indians far beyond tribal agents and commissioners to the desk of the President of the United States, halls of Congress, and into the deliberations of General Conventions of the Episcopal Church. Whipple pressed the buttons that energized the Episcopal Church to a highly visible advocacy role which by the late 1800s was unmatched by other denominations of the Christian church.

When the war to abolish slavery ended, the nation launched into a frenzy of westward expansion. At the same time that the huddled masses of the poor and oppressed of Europe were welcomed to the American shores, the American Indians were systematically and ruthlessly robbed of our land and lifestyle. Land hungry farmers, exploiters and speculators demanded further Indian removal or outright extermination. The-only-good-Indian-is-a-dead-Indian mindset prevailed and the Indian Service, housed until 1849 under the Department of War, was inconceivably corrupt.

Such was the national climate when Whipple strode into an Episcopal Board of Missions meeting in 1866 in New York City. He wrote:

The Board had made no appropriations for Indian missions. A friend offered a resolution to express cordial sympathy with the Bishop of Minnesota, in his efforts to carry the Gospel to the Indian race.

I had just come from Indian Country, where I had witnessed its sorrows and degradation, and was ill from exposure. . .I arose in response to this resolution and said, "If the object of this resolution is to help Indians, it's not worth the paper on which it's written. If it is to praise the Bishop of Minnesota, he does not want it.

"It is an honest fight, and if any one wants to enlist, there is room. . ."

A resolution was then passed initiating action and setting the stage for an astonishing acceleration of the Episcopal Church's Indian work. The next decades saw clergy and laity organized more effectively than in any other denomination to work for reform in Indian affairs.

In 1871 the government, after negotiating some 650 treaties with the various tribes, decreed an end to treaty-making. An ineffectual man, Ulysses S. Grant, was President. General George Armstrong Custer, driven by presidential ambitions, was on a rampage in the west. However, the year 1871 saw the Episcopal Church take forward actions in Indian advocacy. The House of Bishops established the missionary jurisdiction of Niobrara for Indian work, an act accepted by General Convention the following year. This non-geographic jurisdiction was assigned oversight for most of the northern plains Indians. A second turning point was marked when General Convention created a Standing Committee on Indian Affairs, and elevated the unit to the same level as all other domestic mission. Named to the committee were six prominent laymen. Its chairman was William Welsh, who was from an eminent Philadelphia family which would further distinguish itself through Herbert Welsh, a young humanitarian instrumental in founding the Indian Rights Association, advocacy organization from 1882 until the present.

Indians apportioned to various denominations

Whipple and other leaders of the Episcopal Church were proponents of President Grant's controversial "peace plan." Initiated by the Quakers, the peace plan included a church-related Board of Indian Commissioners and William Welsh was named as the board's chairman. The plan placed churches in control of Indian affairs. A goal was to reform the corrupt Indian Bureau by placing committed Christians in direct contact with the tribes. The primary motive, however, was avoidance of further Indian wars rather than altruism for the indigenous peoples.

The second tier of Grant's program was the outright apportionment of Indian tribes to various Christian denominations. Indians were provided no choices. Denominations were alloted various tribes to "Christianize and civilize." The 1872 apportionment assigned the Episcopal Church primary responsibility for the Dakota, with lesser work among the Shoshone-Bannock in Wyoming territory and the Ponca in Nebraska. When the system was fully established, the following divisions existed:

Denomination	Number of Agencies	Number of Indians
Methodist	14	54,473
Orthodox Friends	10	17,724
Presbyterian	9	38,069
Episcopalian	8	26,929
Roman Catholic	7	17,856
Hicksite Friends	6	6,598
Baptist	5	40,800
Dutch Reformed	5	8,118
Congregationalist	3	14,476
Christian	2	8,287
Uniterian	2	3,800
American Board	1	1,496
Lutheran	1	273

Churches were to appoint Indian agents and receive federal funding for operation of mission schools. There would be no separation of church and state in Indian affairs. The idea was not radically new; as far back as 1819 Congress had voted a permanent "civilization fund" with a $10,000 appropriation which would increase annually. The fund was administered by ABCFM for its mission purposes.

William Welsh in 1870 had visited the various reservations and made a detailed report of his travels and his talks with the chiefs. Welsh made recommendations to the Secretary of the Interior and reported to the Episcopal Church, where he made pleas for missionaries and money. The church responded and three missionary organizations, the Domestic Committee, the American Church Missionary Society and the Indian Hope Association of Philadelphia, all turned over monies from their treasuries to Welsh's Indian board.

In an incredibly brief time — 1871 until 1882 — the Episcopal Church sent out 80 new missionaries to Indian country and ordained 20 Indians to the diaconate and two to the priesthood.

The government looked to the churches to transform its Indian agencies into missionary outposts, to send strong honest men as agents, and committed men and women as teachers. Corruption would cease, the political sinecures would disappear, and furthermore, the Indian would be "civilized." That was the dream. Utopia proved illusive; political pressures did not dissolve and the various missionary societies were not prepared to handle the tremendous responsibilities suddenly thrust upon them. Though funding flowed from the government, it was insufficient. By 1882 all the churches had withdrawn from responsibility of agency operation. However, the apportionment system was well established and it has cast a long shadow.

Though the bishop of Minnesota was a strong advocate for the Indians, he, too, presupposed that for an Indian to be a Christian he must cut his hair, wear shoes, get behind a plow and wholly subscribe to the white man's tenets regarding private property. Most of all, presupposed the bishop — along with the overwhelming majority of 19th century Christians — that the "little red brother" must firmly renounce all trappings of "pagan" spirituality. It is ironic that Whipple also stated in his autobiography:

> *I have never known an atheist among North American Indians...They believe unquestioningly in a future life. They believe that every thing in nature — the laughing waterfall, the rock, the sky, the forest — contains a divinity.*

While the bishop's out-of-diocese travel was incredibly extensive, the Whipple years brought notable growth in both white and Indian mission work of the Episcopal Church in Minnesota. Strong, committed church leaders appeared. These included Joseph Alexander Gilfillan, born in Ireland, whose ministry among the Ojibwa at White Earth Reservation was to extend over 25 years. He traveled up and down the country on foot and pony-back and by canoe, and came to speak the language better than any other white man. He gathered around him young Indian men and trained them for the work of ministry among their fellows, made a regular 300-mile circuit of his missions in all seasons and weathers, designed and built little churches, won woodsmen to temperance, started children's boarding schools, and safe-guarded Minnesota forests from destruction. One of his notable works was translation of the prayer book into the Ojibwa language. His language teacher had been Enmegahbowh.

"Straight-Tongue"

As for Whipple, throughout his ministry he remained insistent in his demands for Indians' rights, urging the government to fulfill its promises that Indian land be protected against the encroachment of unscrupulous whites, that Indians be given a voice in their affairs. "Straight-Tongue" was a name given him by the Ojibwa, because, as one said, "he has never spoken to us falsely."

49

When Whipple died in 1901, Enmegahbowh wrote:

> *Our bishop was all love. He preached always, from the beginning: Love, love, love. Love the Great Spirit, love one another, love all other tribes. His one great aim has been to unite us by close connection, Indians and whites, in Christian fellowship.*

Whipple is buried on the grounds of the Cathedral of our Merciful Savior in Faribault, the first building erected in the Episcopal Church as a cathedral. He was not without characteristics of cultural imperialism. He stoutly supported the reservation system; he required his charges to accept the European interpretation of Christianity. His 562-page autobiography is not without ethnocentrism. His references to "our little red brother" do not endear him to the 20th century Native American. Yet, the book provides cherished glimpses of character, humor and wisdom of Indian people of that era. For instance, the bishop tells a story in his autobiography about visiting the Lower Sioux Agency. It was during the Civil War, shortly after the battle of Gettysburg. The bishop arrived at the agency and was taken aback to find a scalp dance in progress. He immediately confronted Wabasha, hereditary chief of the Santee. The Christian chief agreed it was inappropriate for the Dakota to celebrate the taking of a scalp of a Winnebago horse thief caught in the act. The bishop described what followed:

> *...the chief was smoking, but took his pipe from his mouth, and slowly blowing a cloud of smoke into the air said, "White man go to war with his own brother; kills more men than Wabasha can count all his life."*

Enmegahbowh survived his beloved bishop by only nine months. Other Indian clergy would follow Enmegahbowh in the Diocese of Minnesota — Thomas Rouillard, a Santee Sioux, was ordained to the diaconate in 1925; Edward C. Kah-O-Sed, a Canadian-born Ojibwa, in 1926. Kah-O-Sed made a new translation of the prayer book and hymnal into the Ojibwa language and was an inveterate traveler on behalf of the church across northern Minnesota. But it is Enmegahbowh who is most revered by the 11 native clergy of the diocese today. He spent 44 years in service to his church and his people.

Enmegahbowh is buried on White Earth Reservation at St. Columba's. His grave is marked by a gray granite stone for which Congress appropriated funds in acknowledgement of his role as conciliator in the 1862 conflict. Today's Minnesota Committee on Indian Work has added his name to their calendar of saints. St. Columba's had defied time and circumstance, continuing without interruption though its congregation in 1880 was forced to depart on another Trail of Tears 100 miles to the northwest to the White Earth Reservation. Today's St. Columba's, with a seating capacity of 400, is built on a divide on the great forest and vast prairie. A magnificent native stone building, erected in 1881, was destroyed by fire within the past decade, but the original structure was duplicated in rebuilding. Priest-in-charge at St. Columba's is Doyle Turner, who in 1985 became the first Ojibwa to earn the master of divinity degree from Seabury-Western Theological Seminary

The legacy lives

An imprint of countless committed Christian men and women, Indian and white, is stamped upon the history of the Episcopal Church in mission among the Ojibwa and Dakota people in Minnesota. The Diocese of Minnesota of the late 20th century has faithfully followed their example. A contemporary roll call would include an Ojibwa, the Rev. George Smith, who was first chairman of The National Committee on Indian Work (1969); Bishop Robert M. Anderson, who resonates to Indian-articulated priorities; and a highly energetic non-native, Dr. Howard Anderson, who for a decade has creatively framed initiatives in Indian ministry. The latter was largely responsible for the launching of the Native American Theological Association, a consortium of several Christian denominations, to address an acute shortage of Native American clergy. The roll would also include as central to founding Minnesota Committee on Indian work (MCIW) — the Rev. Virgil Foote, the Rev. Doyle Turner, the Rev. Gary Cavender, Dan Brown, Lois Goodwin Olson, Dottie Bluestone, Robert Roy and the late Rev. Marvin Red Elk.

The MCIW is nationally recognized as a diocesan model not only for its program but for its trail-blazing endeavors in reconciliation. MCIW underscores compatibilities of native spirituality and the Christian faith. Many of its leaders participate in traditional Dakota vision quests, sweat lodge and healing ceremonies. Additionally, MCIW has achieved a harmonious working relationship between reservation and urban Indian communities as well as between historic rivals, the Dakota and the Ojibwa. MCIW also has brought together various Christian denominational leaders to provide support to each other, share resources and provide an Indian community voice in the Twin Cities. MCIW is breaking ground for a new model of ecumenical Indian ministry which is affordable, offers a critical mass of Indian Christians, and serves as a laboratory for liturgical renewal which includes Native spiritual and cultural strength.

With their bishop as their broker, MCIW has consistently given leadership to the whole diocese in areas of planning, movement toward total ministry, and stewardship, at last breaking out of the dependency syndrome long linked with Indian Christians. Indian people serve on all major commissions and committees of the diocese and several serve on commissions of the national church. Though today's progressive strategy in Indian ministry in Minnesota evolved from the old missionary model which was blind to Indian beliefs, there is now a new examination of these old values and concepts.

At a tri-diocesan Indian convocation in the summer of 1987, Episcopal Indians from Minnesota, North Dakota and the Diocese of Eau Claire joined non-Indian church people at the cathedral in Faribault and on the great lawn of Shattuck School. The Primate of the Episcopal Church was among the 650 people present to worship, ordain an Ojibwa to the dioconate — Johnson Loud Jr. — and commemorate a spirit of reconciliation in the 125th summer following the tragic Dakota conflict.

The Dakotas: the people, the land and the Episcopal mission

In the 1860s, when few spoke out in behalf of Indians, a voice which did speak out belonged to a young eastern Episcopal clergyman. This rector of a Pennsylvania parish was visiting on the shores of Lake Superior one summer when he saw a crudely-lettered sign:

$250 REWARD
FOR THE HEAD OF A DEAD SIOUX INDIAN

The young clergyman immediately wrote his parishioners back home informing them of conditions of Indians he had witnessed, saying:

I saw numbers of them every day. Sometimes they were picking berries in the woods, sometimes lounging about the streets. They wandered about like sheep without a shepherd. People seem to be concerned about only one thing: these people's extermination. They call now upon you for help.

The young man did not realize it, but was entering a plea for what would become his flock. He was William Hobart Hare. His charge, beginning in 1873 would be the great Sioux nation, and his episcopacy would be the nongeographic jurisdiction called Niobrara, named for a river flowing out of northeast Nebraska into the Missouri.

For the next century, Episcopal mission and ministry would be heavily centered in what would become, in 1883, the Diocese of South Dakota. The diocese today accounts for almost half of all Native American Episcopal communicants. Nongeographic Niobrara Deanery now has 86 chapels dotted across the vast reservation prairies, and many of these white frame chapels date back to the era of Hare and Samuel Hinman, the first Episcopal missionary to bring the gospel among the Sioux.

The Episcopal Church arrived among the once-nomadic, numerous and proud Lakota/Dakota people to witness their diverse bands in the last throes of resistance to the American republic's doctrine of manifest destiny. The role of the Episcopal Church among the Sioux in their painful transition from warrior to ward was riddled with paradoxes. it was an era which saw, on the one hand, benevolent outpouring of money from distant Eastern parishes and organizations for purposes of missionizing, Christianizing and "civilizing" the Sioux. On the other hand, paternalism was preordained, dependency was established, and ethnocentrism was the unstated policy. At the same time the Episcopal Church was spearheading reform in the incredibly corrupt federal Indian bureau, one of its priests, who would eventually head all Indian work in South Dakota, sat in an official capacity with a federal commission that stole the Black Hills, a land long sacred to the Sioux and subsequently, upon discover of gold, sacred to the white man.

At the time of early European contact the various bands of the Sioux were ranging from the Great Lakes area westward. A hunting and warrior society, the Sioux nation was composed of several subtribes or bands which included Hunkpapa, Minneconjous, Yanktonnais, Brule, Blackfeet, Sans Arc, Oglala, and Oohenonpa or Two Kettles.

A treaty in 1825 affirmed the Dakota domain over the vast northern plains extending from the Mississippi River to the Rocky Mountains. Each successive treaty reduced that domain. When Episcopal mission arrived in South Dakota in 1863, the Sioux still held vast territory spilling into Montana, Nebraska, Wyoming and the Dakotas. But with western expansion of white settlers, railroads, and wanton slaughter of the buffalo — primary source of food, clothing and shelter for the Sioux — the bands had clustered around the headquarters of federal Indian agents. Treaties, which ceded the hunting lands, guaranteed the tribes food supplies and cash payments (annuities) that generally arrived late or not at all. With inevitable capitulation to the white invader and the reservation system fully pressed upon them, the bands subsequently came to be identified primarily by names of their reservations — Rosebud, Standing Rock, Brule, Crow Creek, Cheyenne River, Yankton, Sisseton-Wahpeton, and Santee. Only the nearly indomitable Oglala, assigned the Pine Ridge Reservation, managed to retain their Oglala band identification. As to the distinction among the Dakota, the Lakota, and the third differentiation, Nakota, it is a matter mostly of language or dialect as well as the part of the country where the three major bands were living at early European contact. The Dakota were to the east, the Nakota were northern residents, and the Lakota were the western band.

Episcopal mission arrives with exiled Santee

The Connecticut-born, Seabury Divinity School-educated Samuel D. Hinman brought the Episcopal mission among the Sioux, traveling with the pitiful band of Santees exiled from Minnesota in 1863. Virginia Driving Hawk Sneve describes the exodus and westward arrival of the Santees:

They reached Crow Creek on May 30th, and in a matter of days, the hills around the agency were covered with the graves of women and children who had died as the result of the over-crowding on the small boat, and who had no medical attention on their arrival at Crow Creek. The situation at Crow Creek was one of the worst ever inflicted on prisoners in the United States.

It was a horrible region, filled with the petrified remains of the huge lizards and creeping things of the first days of time. The soil is miserable: rain rarely ever visits it. The game is scarce, and the alkaline waters of the streams and springs are almost certain death.

The Indians arrived too late to plant crops, which would not have produced enough harvest in that arid land to support them. The government had to feed them and this was difficult because of the distance from the source of supply.

The Rev. Samuel Hinman joined the Santee at Crow Creek and traveled with them when they were again moved to the mouth of the Niobrara River in Nebraska. This time, they journeyed overland and arrived on June 11, 1866, to a hostile reception from white settlers in the area whose lands had been appropriated by the government for the new Santee reservation.

The Santee, now denied any annuities and forbidden to leave the reservation to hunt, built a log chapel at Bazille Creek under Hinman's direction. He lived among them without any financial aid from the Church Mission Board, and had to rely solely on voluntary gifts from white persons in the East who felt kindly towards the Indians.

In 1864 Mr. Hinman translated a large part of the Book of Common Prayer into the Santee dialect, and it was published in 1865. The Santee came to love the book, as more of them learned to read their own language.

During the time from 1866 to 1868, the chapel at Bazille Creek was used, and the congregation was visited by Bishop Robert H. Clarkson of Nebraska shortly after it was built. In the spring of 1868 the chapel was flooded out, and all records were destroyed.

Through a generous gift from a woman in New Bedford, Massachusetts, a new building was erected. The Chapel of Our Most Merciful Savior was considered to be one of the most beautiful small church buildings in the West.

At about this time, the Rev. Hinman took a small group of the Sioux East, where they impressed the white people in Philadelphia to form an association for the Santee's relief.

Mazakute ordained to priesthood

Hinman in the next decade laid a solid foundation for future Episcopal mission among the Lakota/Dakota. A second station of the Santee mission was built six miles away from Our Most Merciful Savior on land given by Wabasha, hereditary chief and zealous early convert. In 1868, Robert H. Clarkson, bishop of Nebraska, ordained the first full-blooded Dakota, Paul Mazakute (Iron Shooter), as deacon and the next year as priest. For five years Mazakute ministered to his people. He then contracted tuberculosis and had to resign active work but continued ministering. He built a "bough house" for his church, and his rectory was a tepee. Iron Shooter left an account of his work:

> *In 1862 I made my Christian vows. For seven years I was a Catechist, and for five years I have been a Minister. One year I was a Deacon, and for four years I have been a Priest. I went to the Yankton people (1869). Though I have never been far away, yet among Dakotas — at Yankton Agency, and White Swan, and Choteau Creek, at Ponca, at Santee, and on the Bazille — six villages I have proclaimed the glad tidings of the Gospel.*

In Minnesota, one of the two Twin City Indian congregations worships at Mazakute Memorial Mission, a remembrance of the first among many notable Dakota priests.

Immediate impact on Episcopal mission among the Dakota was congressional enactment of the Grant peace plan which apportioned tribes and bands to the various Christian denominations. The Episcopal Church was assigned five Dakota agencies with a population roughly estimated at 14,000. The Episcopal Church was also apportioned the Shoshone-Bannock agency of Wyoming and the small Ponca tribe which, prior to a pitiful subsequent removal, resided in Nebraska.

Both in compliance with terms of the state-church agreement and upon invitation of various Dakota leaders, including Spotted Tail (Sinte Gleska), Episcopal mission was soon to spread. Funding was primarily through intense efforts of William Welsh, the Philadelphia philanthropist and distinguished Episcopal layman.

Hare consecrated as bishop of Niobrara

In 1872, General Convention created the Indian Missionary District of Niobrara. On nomination of Bishop Whipple, on All Saints' Day, 1872, the secretary for the Foreign Committee of the Board of Missions, William Hobart Hare, was elected bishop of Niobrara. He was the 100th bishop in the American Episcopate.

By saddle and buckboard, Hare came to his new assignment in April 1873, to be greeted by a bitter blizzard. His jurisdiction was not over a territory or a region but over a people, the Sioux nation, the first instance of a racial jurisdiction, an act not repeated until the House of Bishops voted to create Navajoland Area Mission in 1977.

For almost 40 years, Hare worked among the Dakota. When he died in 1909, there were 100 congregations where there had been nine and 26 Indian clergy where there had been three.

Dakota clergy, who would become the cornerstone of Hare's work, were on hand to greet their new bishop. In addition to Mazakute, who succumbed to tuberculosis within a month after Hare's arrival, Hinman had trained two deacons. They were Daniel C. Hemans, who would soon die in a smallpox epidemic, and Luke C. Walker, who would live and serve until 1933. Ordained to the priesthood in 1878, Walker — a grandson of Chief Sitting Bull — saw the day when every Indian on the Crow Creek Reservation had converted to Christianity. Two other Dakota deacons had died in the decade before the bishop's arrival. One was Philip Johnson Wahpehan, called Philip the Deacon, who was associated with the Yankton Mission. The chapel at White Swan was renamed the Church of Philip the Deacon after his death in a terrible blizzard. The other deacon was Christian Taopi, once a fierce warrior, whose name — Wounded One — was earned when as a youth he had been injured in a Santee-Ojibwa battle in Minnesota.

Also on hand to greet the new bishop were several white clergy who had responded to an earlier appeal for young missionaries to come west to work among "hostile" Indians. While Hinman had the respect of the Indian clergy, he did not get along with the white missionaries, and almost immediately conflict — which would last for nine years — arose between Hinman and Hare. Eventually, the conflict resulted in Hinman's expulsion from the diocese. He died a broken man in 1890 in Minnesota and was buried at Birch Coulee, not far from the spot where his missionary work among the Dakota had begun 31 years previously.

Hare, whom the Indians sometimes called Zitkana Dzahan (Swift Bird), was born in Princeton, New Jersey, the son of a clergyman and grandson of Bishop John Henry Hobart of New York, who had rekindled mission among the Oneidas after the American Revolution. Hare was described as a man of scholarly tastes, finesse and cultivation; his friends felt his place to be in "centers of learning, not in the destitute and dangerous west among hostile Indians."

The bishop himself described his initial feelings about his Dakota charges:

These Sioux Indians are heathens, heathens not far off but lying cold on the Church's bosom. Our people have seen them lying dead — they have not pitied them but have beaten and stamped on their dead humanity.

God is "Wakantanka"

Driving Hawk, in her history of the Diocese of South Dakota, succinctly characterized the appeal of the Episcopal Church to the Sioux. In her chapter entitled "God is 'Wakantanka'," she says:

> *Religion permeated every aspect of the Dakotas' life. It was impossible to differentiate between the social, economic, and religious phases of the Dakota culture. Religion was inextricably interwoven with every pattern of individual behavior.*
>
> *The early missionaries insisted that their converts repudiate the most basic elements of their culture. To the Dakota, a man was destined to be a warrior and hunter. To refuse to fight or hunt and agree to plow the land was a sign of weakness. The male who voluntarily submitted to these shameful things — which he must do to become a Christian — made great personal sacrifices in the face of degrading ridicule from his people. Women became the first converts, for their acceptance of Christianity did not mean an abandonment of their former role as wife and mother.*
>
> *The Dakotas' acceptance of Christianity was at first an acceptance of the God of their conquerors and a search for the white man's power, without completely abandoning the old beliefs. The missionaries attempted to make it easier to reconcile the different beliefs by calling the Christian God 'Wakantanka,' the Dakota name for the Great Spirit.*
>
> *The color and richness of the Episcopal ritual appealed to the Dakotas, because they could associate such with their native ceremonies. Feast Days and holidays were important in the Church, and provided festivities to a people who needed diversion to relieve the drab drudgery of their days.*
>
> *In addition, the Church had ceremonies for the transition from one stage of life to another, which the Dakota could relate to their native ceremonies. Baptism for the babies and confirmation for those who were passing into adulthood were acceptable substitutes for the Hunka and Puberty rites. The service of the Burial of the Dead had within it the proper honor and mystery which the Dakota gave in their old funeral ceremonies. The Church also permitted the giveaway and final feast given by relatives of the deceased to be held in church guild halls.*
>
> *It was unfortunate that the early missionaries believed that the Dakota had to change his entire way of life to become a Christian [instead of] using the native religion as a frame of reference instead of trying to eradicate it.*

The early Episcopal missionaries were criticized by the more puritanical Calvinistic churchmen for being "lax with their Indian charges. . .allowing them to continue some of their old practices, such as placing food on the graves of the dead." Before the end of the century, however, a less tolerant breed of Episcopal missionaries arrived. For instance, Edward Ashley, who arrived among the Sioux as a carpenter and rose professionally to become archdeacon of Niobrara, chaired an ecumenical committee which outlawed Indian dances. The English-born Ashley became a teacher at Yankton Mission, was sent by Hare to Seabury Divinity School, and was ordained to the priesthood in 1878.

Theft of the Black Hills

Though Ashley is credited in the old Episcopal *Spirit of Missions* publication with "understanding the Indians far better than any white man," according to old newspaper clippings, he counted as his friend George Armstrong Custer. A story in *The Church at Work,* October, 1923, tells of the celebration on the occasion of the archdeacon having completed 50 years of ministry among the Sioux:

> *He is the sole white survivor of that group which framed the treaty of 1876 and opened the Black Hills to white settlers, stripped the Indians of their hunting grounds and led to the Custer massacre of the Little Big Horn.*

Hare, however, is on record in a letter to President Grant opposing the 1874 expedition led by General Custer to explore the Black Hills to ascertain whether rumors were true that there was "gold at the roots of the grass." Custer led 1,200 troops into the Black Hills in direct opposition to terms of the 1868 treaty. Hare informed the President that he feared the expedition would

> *. . .provoke an Indian War and would seriously imperil the existence of the struggling but numerous missions, which encouraged by your (Grant's) policy, the Episcopal Church is nourishing among the Sioux, and endanger the lives of her missionaries.*

Gold, of course, was discovered in the Black Hills. No power on earth could then stop the onslaught of greedy white prospectors or the last desperate assault of the Plains Indians on a Montana creek called Little Big Horn. Literature of half a century after Sioux Victory Day, June 25, 1876, tells of pious pique of white clergy when the victors rode home from Little Big Horn.

One hundred and three years after the Sioux lands, including the Black Hills, were taken, the Supreme Court ruled the seizure to be illegal and stressed the "ripe and rank dishonorable" dealings surrounding the seizure.

In 1987 the Niobrara Convocation and the National Committee on Indian

Work of the Episcopal Church endorsed federal legislation which would return government-owned lands of the Black Hills to the Sioux nation. In the last century when the land was illegally seized the Episcopal Church raised no hue and cry.

A pitiful postscript to Sioux Victory Day and Black Hills seizure was written in 1890 at another creek, Wounded Knee, on the Pine Ridge Reservation, when the Seventh Cavalry slaughtered at least 149 half-starved Minniconjou, struggling through a bitter December morning to reach the Pine Ridge agency for rations. Nearby, Christmas greens were still hanging at the Episcopal Church of the Holy Cross, and the Episcopal ministers and congregation cared for the wounded and buried the dead — 30 soldiers and 20 Indians. The other dead Indians, mostly women and children, were buried on a hilltop in a mass grave. *Spirit of Missions,* in fusty but nonetheless revealing language, in a 1924 article written by the Rev. Nevill Joyner states:

> *What people inhabit the Pine Ridge Reservation? The Oglala band of the Great Sioux Nation, the most war-like of all American Indians and the last to submit to the dominion of the white man. Their last battle was fought on Wounded Knee creek in Pine Ridge. At that time the church at the Indian Agency was used as a hospital and the United States soldiers who fell in battle were given burial in the Episcopal cemetery.*

Trigger-happy Seventh Cavalry troopers acted to avenge the death of Custer and nip further spread of the Ghost Dance religion. Of this messianic movement, which swept across western Indian country, promised the return of the buffalo and departure of the whites from the land of the Dakota, Bishop Hare wrote:

> *A delusion has taken possession of the wilder elements among the Indians. The leaders in the movement have invigorated old heathen ideas with snatches of Christian truth and have managed to excite an amount of enthusiasm which is amazing. They teach that the Son of God will presently appear as the avenger of the cause of the wild Indian.*

When the eighth bishop of South Dakota, Craig Anderson, arrived in his jurisdiction in 1984, he shortly decreed participation of all non-Indian clergy in Lakota/Dakota culture, history and language seminars taught by Indian clergy. As recently as 1926, funds for support of Niobrara Deanery programs which were raised at the traditional Sioux dances were pontifically declined.

Hare's chapels, churches, clergy and schools

By 1885 Episcopal chapels, churches and schools were sprinkled across the nine Sioux Reservations. Many of the chapels yet stand — in virtual isolation from a settlement, a village, a stream or a tree — and on Sunday mornings their bells peal out across the prairies summoning to worship fourth, fifth and sixth generation Sioux Episcopalians. Mainstay at today's chapels are commissioned licensed lay readers, because the 20 Dakota clergy often serve three or four congregations and appear only once or twice monthly to celebrate the Holy Eucharist.

From the beginning of work among the Dakota people, the Episcopal missionaries founded schools. No sooner had Hare unpacked than he had inaugurated the boarding schools, believing value would be gained in "isolating the children from heathen influences." He also justified the boarding school system with a conviction that the church had responsibility not only to Christianize the Indians but to train them in practical ways to prepare for their future — whatever that would be. The government cooperated — its hidden agenda was complete acculturation — and stipulated that rations would be issued only to those children who regularly attended school. Before his first anniversary as diocesan, Hare had founded St. Paul's for boys and St. Mary's for girls. It was not until September, 1986, that St. Mary's, the last of the Episcopal Indian boarding schools, ceased operation.

Hare looked to the boys' boarding schools as a supply source for church leadership. He felt that only by the aid of its own members could a people be effectively evangelized, and he chose men who first became helpers, then catechists, and after training, deacons and priests. For decade after decade, the brightest young men on the Sioux reservations, who in an earlier time would have been hunters and warriors, had three career choices: teach, preach or work for the Bureau of Indian Affairs (BIA). And many became priests. Following the footsteps of Mazakute, in the early years, were three who would serve their church and their people for a half a century. They were Luke C. Walker, Amos Ross and Philip J. Deloria.

Magnificent Lakota/Dakota names appear on clergy rosters of the Diocese of South Dakota. Clergy and catechists listed in a 1937 roster included the names of Brings the Pipe, Charging Cloud, Winter Chaser, White Plume, Standing Elk, Driving Hawk. A priest, Christian B. Whipple, was named to honor the first bishop of Minnesota. In 1987 the roster included American Horse, Bearsheart, Broken Leg, Medicine Eagle, Noisy Hawk, Two Bulls and Two Hawk. The name, however, which stands out above all others among Lakota/Dakota clergy is that of Deloria, a name which for almost a century has notably appeared on the diocese's clergy roster.

The legendary Delorias

Philip J. Deloria, whose Dakota name was Tipi Sapa (Black Lodge), was chief of the Yankton Sioux. Ordained in 1892, he served 40 years on the Standing Rock Reservation. His son, Vine V. Deloria, also served his church and his people for 40 years and retired as archdeacon of Niobrara Deanery.

The story of the conversion of Philip Deloria has become legend. Virginia Driving Hawk Sneve's account is:

> *Tipi Sapa was riding by a chapel (at Greenwood) in full war regalia when he heard the congregation singing, "Guide Me, O Thou Great Jehovah," and he stopped to listen to the words. He did not enter the chapel but rode back later another day to hear the same hymn being sung. Apparently a great impression was made on the young chief. He had understood the words as the hymn was being sung in Dakota. Finally he went to Bishop Hare and stated he wanted to become a Christian. The Bishop told him he must give up his chief's position and cut his hair and become a simple man. Tipi Sapa refused to do this, stating he was a powerful chief. He returned later, however, and was baptized.*
>
> *After his conversion, Philip was sent to Shattuck Military School, Faribault, Minnesota, by Bishop Hare who sensed the young man's leadership potential. At Shattuck, Philip was a special student who concentrated on learning English and mathematics. After his graduation, he returned to Dakota, became a catechist, and then was ordained deacon at St. Stephen's chapel on the Cheyenne River reservation. He was sent to establish St. Elizabeth's school, and after his ordination to the priesthood, became superintending presbyter of the Standing Rock Reservation.*
>
> *After 40 years on the Standing Rock, Philip returned to the Yankton reservation in 1925, and the Church built a home for him at White Swan. In recognition of his devotion, his figure was included among the 98 "Saints of the Ages" in the reredos of the high altar of the National Cathedral in Washington, D.C. He was one of three Americans so honored.*

Besides his son, the archdeacon, Philip Deloria left other descendants of distinction. They have included a daughter, Dr. Ella Deloria, who became a noted scholar, and a grandson, Vine Jr., who is recognized as one of the foremost American Indian authors of the 20th century.

First American Indian Episcopal bishop

Ninety-nine years after the consecration of the bishop of Niobrara, William Hobart Hare, a Santee Sioux was elected to the episcopate as 670th in the line of succession. This first American Indian bishop — Harold Stephen Jones — was born at Mitchell, South Dakota, December 24, 1909; educated at Seabury-Western Theological Seminary; ordained to the diaconate in 1938 and to the priesthood in 1941, and consecrated bishop on January 9, 1972.

61

Upon returning to South Dakota after seminary, Jones served stations, chapels and churches on the Pine Ridge and Cheyenne River reservations, at Wahpeton in North Dakota, and three years among the Navajo at Good Shepherd Mission in Fort Defiance, Arizona. Illness required an early retirement in 1976.

Jones, who had been reared at Santee, tells of his early assignments after graduation from Seabury at age 29. The superintending presbyter, Nevill Joyner, informed him that pay would be $40 a month and that the young clergyman would serve three chapels located 23 miles apart. Jones asked how he was to travel between mission stations. "Walk," pronounced Joyner.

The tall and distinguished bishop tells a story about how he arrived at his first clergy assignment, Christ's Church, Red Shirt Table, on the Pine Ridge Reservation. "I caught a ride on a watermelon truck," he said. "I sat in back among the watermelons in the rain." The rectory at Red Shirt Table, which yet stands, was a tiny one-room cottage to which Jones brought his bride, the beautiful and gracious Blossom. "Our first home was furnished with 21 apple crates," said Mrs. Jones. "We had no electricity or water for the first eight years after Harold was ordained." [His reminiscences are included as appendix V.]

The Niobrara Cross

Early in his tenure, Hare designed a symbol of confirmation among Dakota people — the Niobrara Cross. In the early days, few of the converts could read, so certificates of baptism and confirmation meant little. The bishop recognized the Indian cultural use of symbols and designed the Niobrara Cross with four tepees, symbolizing the four winds. On top of each tepee is a cross. In the very center of the cross are Christ's words, "I am come that ye may have life." Since 1873 every Indian has received the Niobrara Cross at confirmation as a symbol of the truth found in Christianity. In 1975 the Niobrara Convocation voted to share the Niobrara Cross with non-Indian confirmands of the diocese. This cross is now also the symbol of the unity of the two cultures of the diocese.

Niobrara Convocation: a distinct institution

Set into motion prior to Hare's arrival was the Niobrara Convocation, the single most distinctive institution of American Indian Episcopalians. The first Niobrara Convocation was held in October, 1870, at the Church of Our Most Merciful Savior on the Santee Reservation.

Since then, with rare interruptions, the summer gathering has been held annually. President and Mrs. Calvin Coolidge attended the 1927 Niobrara Convocation at Pine Ridge. He appears to have been routinely silent; he is not quoted.

The character of Niobrara Convocation is described by Virginia Driving Hawk Sneve:

The Niobrara Convocation, although it has no Indian ceremonies with it, has served the same social function as the old Sun Dance, when friends and relatives came together in the summer from all directions. The convocation custom of the Indians from the different reservations camping together was not unlike the traditional affairs held in the camp circle each summer by the various tribes.

In 1920 four thousand Dakota assembled at the Santee site for the 50th Niobrara Convocation. A thousand tents dotted the hillside, sloping north to the Missouri River. That encampment was remembered 66 years later by two Sioux clergymen, now retired, who returned to the Church of Our Most Merciful Savior in the summer of 1986 for the 114th Niobrara Convocation, attended by 500. The two elders laughed, and joked, and told stories about the convocation herald in 1920 who rode horseback around the encampment and with his long wooden lance nudged stragglers into meeting sessions. These two, who sat straight on the backless wooden benches under a vast arbor — an open-sided pavilion roofed with boughs — are among the most revered Indian clergy of the Episcopal Church. The elder was Vine Deloria Sr., born in 1901; the younger was Harold Stephen Jones, born in 1909.

At the 50th Niobrara Convocation, five Sioux men were ordained deacons; at the 114th, the first Native American couple was ordained together. Charles and Cheryl Montileaux of Pine Ridge were made deacons by the Rt. Rev. Craig Anderson, and at the ordination, Naomi, the five-year-old daughter of the Lakota couple, carried a thurible filled with sweet grass, the burning of which is a part of a Plains Indian tradition.

The 115th Niobrara Convocation: 1987

At the 115th convocation in June, 1987, Charles Montileaux was priested, and present for the laying on of the hands were 119 priests of the church, including the Presiding Bishop. More than 2,100 were present for the meal which followed the final Eucharist of the convocation, held deep in the Rosebud Reservation at the village of Mission, with two small motels and population of less than 900.

The Presiding Bishop stood in the center of a great circle of American Indians in the twilight of the longest day of the year on the grounds which had been the Bishop Hare School for Indian Boys, and in solemn ritual — as old as time among the peoples of the plains — Edmond Lee Browning was honored in a name-giving ceremony. The Very Rev. Clyde Estes, Lower Brule Sioux, with drum, dignity, and scriptural reference proclaimed the name of the 24th primate of the Episcopal Church to be Inyan Wichasa, "Man of Rock." The traditional Lakota/Dakota giveaway followed. Browning linked arms with Marie Rogers and Christine Prairie Chicken to do the honoring dance during the ceremony. The bishop was visibly moved as he accepted the many magnificent hand-crafted gifts which included eight star-quilts, a beaded stole, and a chief's head-dress with full-length trail. The latter, in resplendent scarlet, perfectly matched the beaded moccasins which had been presented by the Ven. Noah Brokenleg, senior priest of the Rosebud mission, at Browning's 1986 installation.

Throughout most of an afternoon the Presiding Bishop sat quietly, unattended, on a wooden plank propped by concrete blocks, beneath the brush arbor, and listened to concerns of the people of the grass-roots. He carried communion to an ill and hospitalized 98-year-old Hattie Marcus, who with Thelma Winter Chaser, was accorded elder honors of the convocation. He visited the domestic violence shelter operated by White Buffalo Calf Women's Society in one of the buildings of the Bishop Hare School. He observed a cross-section of reservation life dispirited by neglect.

Respected figures of the Indian world participated in sunset prayers, healing services, hymn singing in both Lakota and English languages. Vine Deloria, who now lives in Tucson, was center of a circle of listeners to his enchanting stories; Dr. Ben Reifel, former Congressman, traveled from Florida to visit with old friends and former constituents; Dr. Helen Peterson of Portland, Oregon, former executive director for the National Congress of American Indians, returned as chair of the National Committee on Indian Work of the Episcopal Church. Other visitors came from the Fiji Islands, Germany, South America, Puerto Rico and 18 states of the union.

During the three-day convocation, 85 persons were confirmed, two received, three baptized, 77 commissioned as lay ministers, and one couple married — Debra Rainbow and Frank Black Tail Deer. Honored were the Rev. Charles Moose, who was retiring, and the Rev. John Lurvey for his many active years with the Brotherhood of Christian Unity. Business meetings produced resolutions calling for return of Black Hills land to the Sioux nation and supporting the Indian Health Care Improvement Act. The Rev. Robert Two Bulls of Rapid City was elected itancan (chairman) of Niobrara Council.

A national coalition of Native American clergy was organized with the Rev. Webster Two Hawk (Rosebud Sioux) designated as chairman; the Rev. James Dolan, rector of Holy Apostles on the Wisconsin Oneida Reservation, as vice-chairman; and the Rev. Ron Campbell (Sisseton-Wahpeton Sioux) as secretary.

In the great Sunday morning procession, hundreds walked down the hill from the beautiful old St. James' Chapel behind colorful banners of many of the 86 reservation chapels as well as the banners of Indian congregations from neighboring dioceses. Three bishops walked in the procession; leading them in stately dignity was the retired Santee suffragan, Bishop Jones. Walking together, in full Sioux headdresses, were the tall and fair diocesan bishop and the sensitive and caring primate, who within the first 18 months of his tenure had participated in Native American gatherings in Navajoland, Oklahoma, Niobrara and Minnesota, had met with the National Committee on Indian Work at Church Center in New York, and had broken all records in the number of American Indians appointed to national church committees and commissions.

The service was held in the open air, beneath the brush arbor. Hymns were sung in Lakota and English. Splendid star-quilts, hung behind the altar, served as the dossal. Browning sat in the rugged hand-made tall chair that had been the chair of Bishop Hare. The Presiding Bishop gently called for reconciliation and harmony; he spoke of his own ministry as one of servanthood as he seeks to understand the concerns and special visions of all the people of God in God's whole creation.

Bishop Anderson proclaimed that the 115th Niobrara Convocation had launched a new beginning of a ministry of interdependence in South Dakota, a new vision in the work of the church — new programs for seminary education, new cross-cultural understanding opportunities implemented. Tangibles are established; for instance, there is no longer differential in the salary of Indian and non-Indian clergy in South Dakota. When Anderson was consecrated, he arrived to find that South Dakota clergy pay ranked 97th in the church. He immediately launched a fund drive which raised over $1 million and the campaign has brought Indian clergy salaries up to parity.

Anderson is chief shepherd to 10,000 baptized Episcopal Sioux, an Indian constituency which outnumbers the non-Indian in the diocese. He is leading his flock out of the shadows of the paternalistic missionary mold into a promising dawn of cultural and spiritual interdependence. He is stoutly challenged to lead non-Indian Episcopalians into a visible stance opposed to the prevailing racism in South Dakota and is especially present in areas bordering the nine reservations. In the Rapid City area, among a segment of non-Indian Episcopalians, there surfaced raging opposition to any federal legislation which would return any portion of the Black Hills to the Sioux, and at a desolate hamlet a few miles outside of the Pine Ridge Reservation, a retail merchant in the summer of 1987 still shamelessly displayed a large painted sign blatantly proclaiming, "No dogs or Indians Allowed."

The North Dakota Mission

Indians evangelized Indians in North Dakota. Buried in crumbling old chronicles are passing references to endeavors of Native people in first introducing to other Native people the gospel along with the rites and doctrines of the Episcopal Church. On two of the four North Dakota reservations, where 100 years later the Episcopal Church still has mission, the good news was first brought by other Indians.

In South Dakota the banner of the Episcopal Church was raised in Indian work. However, the House of Bishops in 1883 re-established North and South Dakota as separate missionary districts, and the North Dakota district was charted to minister to white settlers swarming into the region. Indians were ignored.

The Anglican prayer book was first read in today's Diocese of North Dakota at stations of the powerful Hudson's Bay Company and later at U. S. Army posts scattered across the northern plains to subdue the Indians. There is a brief reference to Indian evangelizing efforts of the Hudon's Bay Company which for a century and a half ruled a vast empire from Hudson Bay to the Rocky Mountains. In 1820 the company dispatched a chaplain to a Red River settlement of Scots in the northern-most reaches of today's diocese. John West, former curate of White Roding, Essex, was alloted an extra 50 pounds annually for work among the Indians, but there is no record on how well he earned his extra stipend. However, there is record that West, after a two-year stay among the Scots, moved to Winnipeg where he started St. John's College, and this institution for generations supplied clergy for North Dakota missions and parishes.

Bishop William D. Walker arrived in 1884 in the Territory of North Dakota to be confronted by meager national church funding and local prejudice against Indians. During 1886-1893 the Episcopal Church allocated, over the entire country, a total of $107,146 for Indian education. The Roman Catholic Church expended $1.5 million, and the Presbyterians allocated $150,000 for a single year. Thus, during the crucial transition era, major opportunity for evangelization among the Natives of the northern plains was lost for lack of funding. The bishop's work in the Turtle Mountains, for instance, had to be funded entirely by money he garnered in bits and pieces from wealthy Eastern parishes.

Prejudice toward Indians was rampant among land-hungry white settlers; a climate of latent hostility prevailed across the plains and was especially keen in the communities bordering the reservations. In fact, a staunch old Chippewa churchman is credited by *Spirit of Missions* for his role in "...preventing a repetition of the Custer massacre in the Dunseith hills."

Rising Sun: the persistent Chippewa of Turtle Mountain

That staunch old Chippewa churchman was Rising Sun, whose name memorialized the fact that he had first seen the light of day just as the sun rose in the east. Sometime in the 1860s he took upon himself a near life-time quest. His quest was to bring the gospel and lasting Episcopal mission to his people, a band of Ojibwa which had moved west from Minnesota into the Turtle Mountains of north central North Dakota. Rising Sun's group is still known as the Turtle Mountain Chippewas.

Rising Sun is first glimpsed in 1869 when he set out in the company of several other chiefs for the White Earth Reservation, located 175 miles away in Minnesota. The party was seeking to recruit an Episcopal missionary. They had heard of the work in Minnesota of the indefatigable Enmegahbowh, who two years earlier had been ordained as the first Native American Episcopal priest. Enmegahbowh was unable to produce a missionary for the Turtle Mountain band and Rising Sun trudged on to Faribault, nearly 300 miles south of White Earth. There he pressed his request for a missionary directly to Bishop Whipple. The Minnesota bishop unfortunately had no one to send but recommended that Rising Sun return to White Earth and prevail upon Enmegahbowh to teach him the creed, the Ten Commandments and the Lord's Prayer.

By 1873 the Turtle Mountain people had made three more fruitless pleas for an Episcopal missionary. The dauntless Rising Sun, despite disappointments, continued his lonely efforts to bring the Christian gospel to his people, and historians provide a will-o'-the-wisp vignette of Rising Sun counting the days, and each seventh day, teaching his people all he had learned from Enmegahbowh.

In 1875 Dr. David Buel Knickerbacker, later bishop of Indiana, appeared in the Turtle Mountains with a treaty commission. His astonishment was considerable when he discovered Rising Sun's followers reciting devotionals from memory. He reported to Whipple that he had discovered "Forty-seven Chippewas trying to be 'good Indians'. . . keeping up prayer and singing. . . but feeling the need for someone to be with them to lead and teach them." The Minnesota bishop was still unable to send a missionary.

Nine years after the Knickerbacker report, a new bishop arrived in North Dakota. He was William D. Walker, noted in later years for his "railroad cathedral" because he used a railroad car to crisscross his large diocese. Rising Sun, then about 60, set out to call on the new bishop. He carefully laid his strategy to succeed in his 15-year quest. As companions he chose his seven-year-old grandson, a young chief named Little Elk, and one of the tribal elders who spoke a little English. Rising Sun also decided to prevail upon Enmegahbowh to accompany the Turtle Mountain emissaries, so first the party made a very long detour to the White Earth Reservation. Enmegahbowh agreed to go with them, and the group set out on an 11-day walk from White Earth to the see city of Fargo. Old documents provide a glimpse of the stalwarts along with description of the clothing they had acquired to impress the bishop:

. . .They had traded beadwork for "civilized" clothing, and one of the group wore checkered trousers, another wore a vest, and the lad wore a long linen duster which trailed the ground. The old chief, Rising Sun, donned a battered white top hat. . .Bishop Walker warmly

*received the emissaries; they are recorded as having enjoyed his cakes
and candies.*

The initial meeting lasted through the night into early morning, and the Chippewas at last wrung from the Episcopal Church a commitment for mission. True to his word, during the ensuing year the bishop from his meager funding erected the Church of the Resurrection at Belcourt. In the following year he sent to the Turtle Mountain Chippewas a teacher, Wellington Jefferson Salt, a Canadian of mixed Indian and white ancestry. Son of a Methodist minister, Salt had been working in Minnesota lumber camps when he made his decision to offer his services to Walker. Salt arrived at the Turtle Mountain Reservation on May 2, 1888. During his first year he enrolled 20 pupils at the school he established at the Belcourt church building. Though he later was engaged to teach at the government school, Salt continued to conduct weekly lay services and at intervals Enmegahbowh traveled the 175 miles from White Earth to administer Holy Communion.

In 1901 an outbreak of smallpox closed the Turtle Mountain government school and Salt was transferred to a South Dakota government school. His departure spelled doom for the Church of the Resurrection and the little building was soon hauled 12 miles away to Rolla, a white community.

Rising Sun, who lived to be about 110, did not even then lose hope for lasting Episcopal mission among his people. From his first government annuity check, he and his wife purchased $30 worth of lumber for a future Episcopal chapel and kept the lumber stored in their tiny hut for six years. He then gave land from his allotment, near Dunseith, for an Episcopal mission. A full decade passed before his gifts were accepted but in 1911 — reckoned to be Rising Sun's 99th year — the faithful old Chippewa saw his dream become reality. Salt was ordained to the permanent diaconate, returned to Turtle Mountain, and on October 15 the Chapel of St. Denys was dedicated. The little chapel, built of logs set upright on the foundation, would soon be renamed St. Sylvan's and it was ably served by Salt until his death in 1920.

Today, St. Sylvan's is potentially North Dakota's largest Indian congregation. It stands on a high elevation of land as a monument to the faith, perseverance and devotion of Rising Sun, who for nearly half a century knocked on Episcopal doors seeking help to bring the gospel to his people and, who in his quest, once donned a battered white top hat to impress a young bishop from New York.

To coincide with the centennial of the first Episcopal mission on the Turtle Mountain Reservation, a revitalized North Dakota Committee on Indian Work has targeted St. Sylvan's for major new emphasis. Short-range goals include placement of a full-time priest at St. Sylvan's, currently served by a part-time, non-Indian priest, with occasional visits by White Earth Chippewa, the Rev. George Smith of Minnesota.

Fort Totten mission

By 1884 the Native peoples of the northern plains were living in poverty in small areas of the reservation. The constricted area of the Chippewas was located in the Turtle Mountains near the Canadian border. Remnants of three tribes, the sparse survivors of smallpox and other European-inducted epidemics, were squeezed onto Forth Berthold Reservation. They were the Arikara, Hidatsa and Mandan, who in the early part of the century had been host to the Lewis and Clark explorers. Additionally, Walker's jurisdiction encompassed several bands of Sioux, both Dakota and Lakota people. At Fort Totten, in the east central part of his district, were the Devil's Lake Sioux, consisting of the Sisseton, Wahpeton and Cut-Head bands. Two other Sioux reservations straddled the North Dakota-South Dakota border. In the far southwest was a small sliver of the Sisseton Reservation, and, west of the Missouri River lay a large part of the huge Standing Rock Reservation.

After launching his initial Indian mission at Turtle Mountain, Walker next turned to Fort Totten and in 1891 established there a chapel and a school in the old military trading post which he purchased when the army detachment was withdrawn. The bishop sent the Rev. William D. Rees to minister to Indian students whom the government gathered up from numerous northern tribes and bands for training at the newly-established, government-operated, industrial boarding school. Soon, Rees, who readily learned the Dakota languages, had as many as 100 students regularly attending his Sunday school. By the end of the century he had baptized 305 Indians and presented 276 for confirmation. He was assisted by a mixed-blood Sioux catechist and postulant for holy orders, John S. Brown.

Today's mission at Fort Totten, St. Thomas, dates back to 1898 when Iyayukamani (He-Follows-Walking) loaned his home for services in the Dakota language. Years later, a woman in Rochester, Minnesota, donated $1,000 to build the Margaret Breckenridge Memorial Chapel on land acquired from Iyayukamani. The chapel, completed in 1923, was initially located atop Raven Hill, but subsequently moved to the town of Fort Totten.

Fort Berthold: Indians evangelize Indians

Two distinguished native priests have served the St. Thomas congregation. William Skala Cross, the first North Dakota Indian to be ordained to the priesthood, worked at St. Thomas in the 1930s. Born on the Standing Rock Reservation, Cross became a lay reader in 1908, was ordained deacon in 1925, and priest in 1928. The esteemed Moses Mountain came from South Dakota to Fort Totten as catechist and, following his ordination in 1954, he was priest-in-charge at Fort Totten until 1957. Then he was transferred to the Fort Berthold congregation of St. Paul's, where he served with distinction until his death in 1984.

At Fort Berthold, again it was an instance of Indians bringing the gospel to other Indians. St. Paul's Mission traces its beginnings to the last year of the last century when a group of 20 Standing Rock Sioux Episcopalians set out far up the Missouri River on a preaching mission to the Arikara people at Fort Berthold Reservation. Leaders of the Indian missionaries were a native deacon, Thomas P. Ashley, and a lay reader, William White Eagle. Likelihood of even a modicum of success could scarcely have been anticipated because Yellow Bear, one of the principle Arikara leaders, not only vehemently opposed all aspects of white civilization, but held a specific hostility toward Christianity. Records fail to provide details, but the Standing Rock missionaries reached the defiant Arikara chieftain, and to the amazement of both the Episcopal Sioux and his fellow tribesmen, Yellow Bear was converted to Christianity. At his baptism he added Paul to his name in honor of the early Christian saint. When a chapel was erected, it, too, honored St. Paul. Paul Yellow Bear throughout the remainder of his life as a lay reader, reinforced the Episcopal presence at Fort Berthold.

Moses Mountain arrived at St. Paul's in the aftermath of a sweeping upheaval which victimized and displaced the Fort Berthold people. In the 1950s a decision was made in Washington to build Garrison Dam across the Missouri River. The gigantic dam was to provide flood protection to down-river white interests. The Indians had no say in the decision. The reservoir eventually inundated the fertile bottom lands of the reservation. Many of the Fort Berthold people slid down the economic scale from stability as small farmers and ranchers to welfare recipients. The communicants of St. Paul's experienced a special wrench; their chapel and cemetery had to be moved from the wooded lowlands to a barren windswept plain overlooking the huge artificial body of water stretching over 100 miles upriver.

With the death of Mountain, St. Paul's at White Shield was served by a part-time, non-Indian priest. However, the mission launched by Indians to Indians looked forward to the ordination of the first Arikara Episcopal clergyman, Duane Fox, a candidate for holy orders under Canon 11 and an officer and leader of the North Dakota Committee on Indian Work.

The Episcopal start at Standing Rock

Indians also had a major role in generating Episcopal mission at the huge Standing Rock Reservation. Two young Dakota students — their names were not recorded — led the way to launching Episcopal mission on the North Dakota side. Along with many other plains Indians, they were sent to Hampton Institute in Virginia for education. While in the east they became acquainted with Episcopal services and the prayer book. Both of today's North Dakota Standing Rock congregations — St. James' at Cannon Ball and St. Luke's at Fort Yates — can trace their beginnings back a century to the return of the young men in 1887 to Standing Rock Reservation, home of Sitting Bull's people, the Hunkpapas.

The students had come into possession of a Dakota translation of the prayer book, likely from Hare's mission at St. Elizabeth's on the South Dakota side of the Standing Rock. The students called the Episcopal chaplain at the military post at Fort Yates, and with his assistance regular services were begun for 50 or more persons. A brief reference to the Standing Rock mission in the history of the North Dakota diocese says:

> *Their chapel was a rude log hut built by one of the group. These native lay readers, after instructing some Indians for baptism sent a letter to Bishop Walker asking him to visit Standing Rock. In the summer of 1891, the bishop went to the reservation and at Cannon Ball baptized 13 persons — three infants, six boys and girls and four adults.*

> *By the summer of 1892, with Chaplain G.W. Simpson of Fort Yates working with them, there were between 125 and 150 identified with the Episcopal Church. Nearby, the Sioux built a long guild house with clay roof and earthen floor. Services, held on Friday, and Sunday, were attended by 100 men and a like number of women.*

While there is no recorded evidence of Walker's further support to the fledgling mission at Standing Rock, note is made that at Cannon Ball — so named because of unique rock formations found in the vicinity — a small frame chapel was erected, partly funded by donations from Trinity Church, Newark, New Jersey. Subsequently, mention is made of the 30 families at Cannon Ball aspiring to build a stone chapel, "but by 1904 their building fund had reached only $6.50."

Then, in 1908, there appeared on the Standing Rock Reservation a remarkable character named Aaron McGaffey Beede, who built with his own hands a church building which "will withstand anything but a number one cyclone." A footnote on the "venerable Beede" — a professor of Greek turned priest — discloses that after long playing the advocate's role in Indian affairs, he was incensed over an incident involving Eastern criticism of the manner in which he distributed shipments of old clothing and goods. It seems that touring Episcopalians in 1916 questioned his distribution of their largess and protested to New York church authorities. The fiery Beede held strong opinions about churchmen who could afford transcontinental vacations yet questioned disposition of cast-off clothing. He resigned in a monumental huff.

Beyond the unknown laity who initiated the Standing Rock mission, an impressive roster of Indian successors can be sketched. First on the list is Thomas P. Ashley who came from South Dakota as catechist and was placed in charge of the Cannon Ball chapel. Later ordained to the permanent diaconate, his career is recorded as having been cut short following divorce in 1907. John S. Brown is listed as a mixed-blood candidate for holy orders. Among others associated with the Standing Rock mission were Charles Prettyflute, Alexander His-War, Martin Prettyfeather (who changed his name to Martin See-Walker, memorializing a visit with the bishop), Paul Bear Paw, Julia Bear Paw, Lucy Shoot-the-Buffalo and William White Feather.

A stand-out early name on the Standing Rock roster was that of Chief Red Hail (said to have been born during a great meteor shower) who was largely responsible for the raising of a third congregation now closed, St. Gabriel's Chapel at Brein. A grandson of Red Hail, William Skala (White) Cross, was the first North Dakota native priest. The name of the Rev. Herbert H. Welsh (who adopted the name of the philanthropist and Indian advocate) was long associated with both St. James' and St. Luke's. In recent times an Oglala from Pine Ridge Reservation, the Rev. Harold Eagle Bull, served the St. James' mission.

In 1969 Innocent Goodhouse, born on the Standing Rock Reservation, became vicar of St. Luke's and continued his ministry until well past the mid-1980s. One of the first graduates of the Dakota Leadership Program, Goodhouse, along with Moses Mountain, is among the distinguished Indian leaders of the diocese in contemporary times.

Vision of future North Dakota mission

The Diocese of North Dakota of the 1980s honors the rich heritage of Native Americans who reside within its realm — the various Dakota bands, the Fort Berthold tribes, the Ojibwas of Turtle Mountain. The bishop of North Dakota, Harold Hopkins Jr., in 1985 became the first Episcopal bishop to "go up the hill" on a traditional Dakota vision quest, and his deep respect for Native American spirituality is symbolized by the eagle feather attached to his bishops' staff. The feather was a gift from Elmer Running, a Lakota medicine man.

Winds of change in Indian ministry sweep across the immense 70,000-square-mile Diocese of North Dakota in which five reservations are located. A sensitive and responsive bishop has raised the North Dakota Committee on Indian Work to a vital decision-making role in coordinating all Native American mission and ministry of his diocese. Instrumental in Indian empowerment is Dr. Howard Anderson who in 1985 was appointed for Indian work for the dioceses of North Dakota and Minnesota. Coordination between the dioceses extends to Episcopal oversight by the North Dakota bishop of some northern Minnesota reservations, plus joint annual convocations, and a new urban ecumenical project in the border cities of Fargo, North Dakota, and Moorhead, Minnesota.

Indian work in the Diocese of North Dakota began with the mission mentality of the past century. During a convocation 50 years ago a resolution was passed voicing opposition to native dances and traditional give-aways. In fact, annual summertime convocations or "coming-together" events were at one time abolished.

The Diocese of North Dakota of the late 1980s was in the forefront of a late-coming response to need for ministry among the Native peoples who have migrated from the reservations into urban communities. In cooperation with the Diocese of Minnesota a new ecumenical ministry has been introduced in the Fargo-Moorhead community in which an estimated 2,500 Indians reside. The new urban Indian project, begun in 1985 in cooperation with Lutherans, has gathered a community of native peoples, provides social outreach, and is a challenge to prevailing racism.

St. Augustine's of Chicago

The mid-1800s was the era of removal; the mid-1900s was the era of relocation. In the 1950s the U. S. government launched programs of "relocating" Indians, that is, moving them from reservations to urban areas, where employment potential appeared brighter. The Bureau of Indian Affairs set up relocation field offices to assist in resettlement, and the first offices of the relocation program were in Chicago and Los Angeles. Later there were BIA offices in 10 other cities including Denver, Dallas, Cleveland and San Francisco.

Serving an extremely valuable service in assisting with transition from rural and reservation environment to urban survival were programs of social outreach sponsored by Episcopal parishes and dioceses. Not only did these programs offer referral and social ministry, they often provided an Indian community gathering place which was of inestimable value to the transplanted Indians in retaining their identity within an alien world.

St. Augustine's in Chicago established an American Indian Center in the 1950s and the program has continued as a social outreach and gathering place. Directed by the Rev. Peter Powell, the program has established a pastoral relationship with the community of Native American students at Seabury-Western Theological Seminary at Evanston.

Nebraska's Jubilee Ministry

St. Mark's in Gordon, Nebraska, 18 miles south of the Pine Ridge Reservation, was designated in 1986 as a Jubilee Center, and has nourished both spiritually and physically a Native American community which had moved from the reservation to the sandhill farm and ranch community of 2,100. Long a supporter of the Sheridan County Lakota Association, a self-help agency for local Native Americans, St. Mark's cosponsored the first Lakota art show in the community's history, which brought nationally-known artists to exhibit their works and encouraged development of a permanent Lakota Cultural Center in Gordon.

The Diocese of Nebraska also maintains a mission congregation on the Winnebago Reservation which serves an estimated 600 baptized Indians.

Diocese of Iowa urban work

Also designated as a Jubilee Center is an urban Indian ministry program in Sioux City, Iowa. For more than 30 years, St. Paul's has maintained an inclusive program for the Native American community. It began in 1954 when the parish started to hold services for Indian people and invited the Lakota/Dakota priests and lay readers from the neighboring South Dakota reservations to conduct the worship services. St. Paul's was established a century ago as a white mission and experienced many financial set-backs through the years. Finally, in 1964 the white congregation merged with other Sioux City churches. The Indian congregation, however, continued at St. Paul's. In 1968 Philip Allen, a Lakota, seminary-trained priest, took charge of a growing St. Paul's and organized the American Indian Center. In the mid-1970s a comprehensive Indian Health Service was added to the social outreach program to serve the large, predominantly Lakota/Dakota urban Indian community. In addition to the health care program, directed by Elaine Provost, the mission offers service referrals, support for youth and substance abuse programs.

Wisconsin Tri-Diocesan Ministry

A ministry of highly visible advocacy to combat a vicious atmosphere of racism and backlash against Ojibwa people is under way in joint endeavors of the three dioceses of Wisconsin. The three bishops in the summer of 1987 issued a joint pastoral letter in support of Indian treaty rights. Signed by William C. Wantland, bishop of Eau Claire; William L. Stevens, bishop of Fond du Lac, and Roger White, bishop of Milwaukee, the letter was issued to all Episcopal congregations in Wisconsin as well to public officials and the press. The statement was in response to the backlash against Indian people after courts upheld hunting and fishing rights retained by the Ojibwas in treaties. The Ojibwa people have struggled for decades to hold the rights reserved by their tribal governments on lands in northern Wisconsin, ceded to the United States in 1871. These rights were upheld in federal court in 1983 in the Voigt decision.

Annually, racial tensions had heightened in northern Wisconsin. 4 hundred protesters appeared in 1987 at a lake community and strained against police lines to hurl racial insults at 50 Ojibwa spearfishers. While pressure groups generated hysteria, there was no threat on the part of the Indians to diminish the deer supply. In 1986 non-Indian bow hunters took around 25,000 deer while Indians took 600. Nevertheless, a Wisconsin congressman introduced a bill which would repeal Wisconsin Ojibwa treaties and a Wisconsin senator issued a special report on treaty rights which appears to seek to circumvent court decisions which favored Indians. Both lawmakers are Episcopalian.

The joint letter of the bishops reminded Episcopalians that the 1985 General Convention had adopted a resolution which urged all agencies of the church to advocate and support the honoring of all Indian treaties.

Sixth-generation Episcopalian Oneidas are instruments to building a new tri-diocesan alliance in Wisconsin. Led by the bishop of Eau Claire, himself a member of the Seminole nation, a coalition for mutual support was organized in 1986. Eau Claire, which has no Indian-predominant congregations, contributed to the coalition its stalwart bishop along with Ojibwa laity representation. The Diocese of Milwaukee, which had presupposed scant Episcopal Indian presence, discovered that 15 per cent of the cathedral congregation are American Indians drawn to the city to find work. A majority of the Indians who worship at the cathedral came from the Oneida nation, where the Episcopal Church has been an integral part of community life since the early 1800s. Holy Apostles, on the Oneida Reservation, has the distinction of being the largest congregation in the Diocese of Fond du Lac.

And so, at last Indian people have begun building our own systems for mutual support for protection against the ongoing onslaught of infringement on inherent and court-affirmed treaty rights, at the same time confronting racism likened to the Ku Klux Klan era in the deep south.

SIOUX LAND CESSIONS

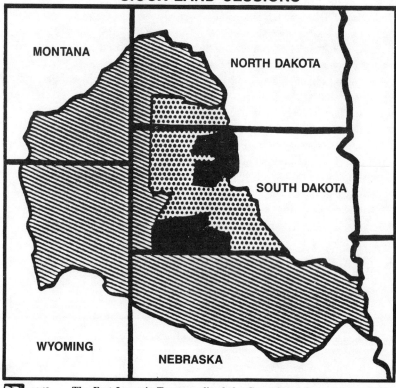

1868 The Fort Laramie Treaty outlined the Great Sioux Reservation and the unceded Sioux territory.

1876 The Great Sioux Nation after the United States illegally took the Black Hills and the unceded Sioux territory.

1889 The Great Sioux Nation after the United States government broke the Nation up into smaller reservations for the various Sioux bands.

Chapter 6

Episcopal mission and ministry among Native Americans of the southwest

In the last two decades of the 19th century, the height of global expansion of Christian mission to distant continents, the Episcopal Church feebly launched two meagerly-funded missions among Indians of the southwest, by then the population center for survivors of manifest destiny. The American Indian population of the United States at the end of the last century totaled less than a quarter-million. More than half of us were among the 67 tribes and bands which had been wedged into Indian Territory, itself to fall prey to land-hungry settlers and railroad empires in the dawn of the new century. The territory would become, in wanton disregard to countless pacts, pledges and promises, the state of Oklahoma.

There is a certain irony about the two solitary missions in the vast southwest. Out of the Oklahoma mission, a century later, emerged the first American Indian saint of the Episcopal Church. In the second, among the Navajo, the Episcopal Church, again a century later, has opportunity to empower indigenous leadership in accord with the Roland Allen model of mission and ministry.

The deacon saint, David Oakerhater

Three hundred and seventy eight years after the King of England affixed his seal on the Jamestown Charter, an American Indian was added to the calendar of saints of the Episcopal Church, symbolically sealing a new covenant of inclusiveness and interdependence with a vision toward reconciliation and wholeness.

> *O God of unsearchable wisdom and infinite mercy, you chose a captive warrior, David Oakerhater, to be your servant, and sent him to be a missionary to his own people, and to exercise the office of a deacon among them: Liberate us, who commemorate him today, from bondage to self, and empower us for service to you and to the neighbors you have given us; through Jesus Christ, the captain of our salvation, who lives and reigns with you and the Holy Spirit, one God, for ever and ever. AMEN.*

Recognition of Oakerhater was pursued untiringly by the late Lois Carter Clark, a member of the Creek nation of Oklahoma, and a woman who gave distinguished service to the Episcopal Church at parish, diocesan and national levels. Two months before her death in 1985, she stood before the 68th

General Convention in Anaheim, California, to express the gratitude of Indians for the recognition, albeit belated, of the Cheyenne deacon. In an air of gracious authority, she presented an icon of Oakerhater to the National Cathedral and blankets to the incoming and outgoing primates of the Episcopal Church.

Oakerhater, whose name roughly translates as Making Medicine, as a young man had distinguished himself for bravery as a member of an elite Cheyenne warrior society. His final moments in the role of warrior were played out on June 24, 1874, in the barren red cedar breaks of the Texas Panhandle at the Battle of Adobe Walls. An almost incredible chain of events and personages propelled the Cheyenne warrior from the battle of Adobe Walls — among the last of a long series of Indian-white confrontations in Texas — to his return to the Cheyennes to build Whirlwind Episcopal Mission, which continues its work today.

Adobe Walls was a camp of white buffalo hunters. The Plains Indians had watched as the once-endless herds of buffalo had wantonly been destroyed. One June sunrise in 1874, 700 warriors of five tribes — Kiowa, Comanche, Wichita, Cheyenne and Arapaho — futilely attacked the camp. With long-range buffalo guns, the hunters methodically picked off the circling warriors. The attack failed. Warrior leaders, including the 30-year-old Oakerhater, were arrested by the U. S. Army; none was allowed a trial. Nine Comanches, 26 Kiowas, 2 Arapahos and 33 Cheyennes, including Oakerhater, were placed in custody of Lieutenant Richard H. Pratt, who would figure prominently in the later life of Oakerhater. Subsequently, the man who in time would be called blessed was hauled away from Fort Sill, Oklahoma, restrained by heavy leg chains in a creaking army wagon, en route to military prison at Fort Marion in St. Augustine, Florida. He would return in 1881 to his people as a deacon. For 50 years, until his death in 1931, he was to serve his church among the Cheyenne. For a dozen years, his was the only ordained Episcopal presence in the Indian Territory.

Born in 1846 or 1847, Oakerhater grew up in a non-white, non-European culture and land. His people, once proud and free, were gradually crushed by the pressure of an alien government which desired the land and even the life of Indian America. Peace loving, the Cheyenne nation was dealt a severe blow in 1864 by Colonel John Chivington, an ordained Methodist minister, and the Colorado Home Guard, in the massacre of Sand Creek. This unprovoked attack slaughtered 140 women and children in the camp, together with some 60 men, under a flag of truce.

Four years later, on a cold Thanksgiving morning, 1868, the Cheyenne survivors were annihilated before dawn by Colonel George Armstrong Custer and the Seventh Cavalry at Washita Village in Oklahoma. Black Kettle, the

Cheyenne peace chief, was killed. Men, women and children were mercilessly slaughtered, the village destroyed, and 900 Indian ponies shot on the spot by order of Colonel Custer. Certain Cheyenne warrior survivors went north to relish victory eight years later on June 26, 1876, on a Montana creek called Little Bighorn.

Early in Oakerhater's prison years, Bishop Henry Whipple of Minnesota is said to have conducted a week-long preaching mission among the imprisoned Indians while on one of his several Florida journeys. To what extent Oakerhater's life was influenced by the bishop in unknown; Lieutenant Pratt, however, is known to have shaped Oakerhater's Christian development.

Connection with Senator George Hunt Pendleton and his wife, Alice, of Cincinnati, was doubtlessly made during the prison years. Likely the link was through archery instruction for the Pendleton daughter when the family visited Florida, and through art. Oakerhater, along with other non-English speaking prisoners began drawing on ledger paper supplied by Pratt. Their art work "talked" not only to whites, but served as communication with people back home. The ledger drawings, an outgrowth of traditional symbol or pictographic art, were to become national treasures and are found today in private collections and several museums, including the Smithsonian. The drawings of Oakerhater bear the name Making Medicine.

Alice Pendleton, the daughter of Francis Scott Key, arranged for Oakerhater to receive a Christian education in upstate New York, where the Episcopal Church, generations earlier, first launched its mission among American Indians. In 1878 Oakerhater began studies under the direction of the Reverend John B. Wicks. In October of that year he was baptized, and later confirmed. At baptism, Oakerhater included the name of Pendleton, to honor his patrons, and embarked upon a three-year theological education under auspices of Deaconess Mary D. Burnham. In 1879 Captain Pratt was named superintendent for a new educational institution in Pennsylvania which would come to be known as Carlisle Indian School. At Pratt's request, Oakerhater returned to Indian country to recruit for Carlisle, and while in the west, he reunited with his wife and small son whom he had not seen since his imprisonment. Oakerhater's family returned to New York with him. Tragically, his family did not survive the cold upstate New York winter of 1880.

On June 7, 1881, David Pendleton Oakerhater was ordained deacon by Bishop Frederic D. Huntington of the Diocese of Central New York. He left immediately for the Cheyenne nation of Oklahoma, in the company of Wicks and a Kiowa deacon, Paul Zotom. In spite of repeated tragedy, imprisonment and injustice, Oakerhater had learned of Jesus Christ from his former enemies, and totally embraced the Prince of Peace. During his first address to the assembled leaders of the Cheyenne nation, Oakerhater declared:

*Men, you all know me. You remember when I led you out to war
I went first and what I told you was true. Now, I have been away
to the East, and I have learned about another Captain, the Lord Jesus Christ, and He is my leader. He goes first, and all He tells me
is true. I come back to my people to tell you to go with me now on
this new road, a war that makes all for peace and where we (ever)
have only victory.*

Within three years, the whole Cheyenne nation was brought to Christ. Early
converts included Wah-Nach, mother of Oakerhater, and Whirlwind, the chief
of the Cheyenne and son of the Cheyenne peace chief, Black Kettle. Located
near Watonga, Oklahoma, a few score miles from the Washita battle site, was
the land alloted to Chief Whirlwind. Around the turn of the century, Whirlwind gave the land to the Episcopal mission, and it has since been known
as Whirlwind Mission of the Holy Family, the religious and education center
for the people. Until World War I, the mission operated a school for the
Cheyenne people, with a deep respect for the Cheyenne way of life. The federal government determined that this way of life was to be suppressed, and
the church, after resisting tremendous government pressure for a number of
years, was forced to close the school in 1917.

Though ill health had forced Wicks to leave the Cheyenne mission after
only three years, and the work founded by the Kiowa, Zotom, soon failed,
Oakerhater continued to work alone, functioning as the Cheyenne peace chief
and "holy man," marrying and burying the faithful, baptizing and preaching
among the population, and training lay readers to carry on the work of Christianity. For 12 years, Oakerhater and his congregation were the Episcopal
Church's only presence in what is now Oklahoma.

Episcopal absence in other Indian Territory mission

Sixty-seven tribes and bands were crowded into Indian Territory in the
removal period, with solemn pledge that the land would be exclusively ours
for "as long as the grass shall grow and the water flow." First to be herded
in incalculable misery on the Trail of Tears were the great southeastern nations,
long called the five civilized tribes — Choctaw, Chickasaw, Cherokee, Seminole and Creek. From Mississippi, Alabama, Georgia, Florida and North
Carolina in the 1830s they came, and with them walked protestant missionaries. Soon to follow to the Indian Territory were people indigenous to the
eastern seaboard and Pacific northwest, from the plains, desert and Great
Lakes. Strong consideration was for a time given to settling the Sioux in the
Indian Territory. With the Indians came preachers and teachers sent by the
Baptists, Methodists, Presbyterians, Mennonites, Reformed, Roman Cathol-
ics, Congregationalists and Quakers.

Jackson Kemper, the first missionary bishop of the Episcopal Church, visited the Indian Territory and came across remnants of Iroquois tribes living along the Neosho River and "still in possession of their faith with Prayer Books given their ancestors by the Society for the Propagation of the Gospel," according to documents of the Diocese of Oklahoma. The documents say Kemper went before a council of the Seneca to ask that a missionary be allowed to work and teach among them, but was refused.

There were at least two Episcopal military chaplains stationed in the Indian Territory who had contact with the Cherokee. Records tell of confirmation in 1844 of

> ...*two Cherokee females, one of them a lady of great respectability and refinement. The other, a young girl, was described as too shy to step forward at the time of confirmation. Finding the girl, 'sobbing bitterly' following the services, Bishop Freeman made haste to arrange for her early confirmation.*

There is also reference in the Oklahoma records to a scholar, linguist and ordained deacon who lived and worked among the Osage people. When the ill-fated Ponca, formerly of Bishop Hare's jurisdiction, were forced to move to the Indian Territory there were among them, without doubt, confirmed Episcopalians. But no records exist of further Episcopal contact.

In 1889 vast lands in Oklahoma Territory were opened for white settlement and by 1893 white "Sooners" had surreptitiously encroached upon the Indian Territory. General Convention created the Missionary District of Oklahoma and Indian Territory and named as its bishop Francis K. Brooke. The bishop began no new specifically Indian mission nor did he ordain the faithful Cheyenne to the priesthood. A 1925 church publication noted there were 120,000 people of Indian blood in Oklahoma, and that they were still a "peculiar" people, but were rapidly being absorbed in the nation.

Episcopal Indian presence in Oklahoma

Some 3,400 of these "peculiar" people are baptized Episcopalians, approximately 15 per cent of the baptized members of the Diocese of Oklahoma. Except for the Cheyenne congregation, they worship in an "integrated" church, and strive to sensitize their pew-mates to Indian issues — treaty rights, sovereignty, culture and history.

The Diocese of Oklahoma Committee on Indian Work has the longest sustained program of the church and has sent forth its Native-born to various leadership roles in the national church. Four Native Oklahomans have served as staff officer for Native Ministries at the Church Center in New York. They are Dr. Howard Meredith, Cherokee; Fayette Knight McAlear, Seneca-Cayuga; the Reverend Steve Charleston, Choctaw; and Owahan Anderson, Choctaw. Additionally, Dr. Carol Hampton, Caddo, began work in the autumn of 1986 as field officer for native ministry and established the national church's field office in Oklahoma City. William C. Wantland, bishop of Eau Claire, Seminole, headed the National Committee on Indian Work for six years. Tim Tall Chief, Osage, has served on the Coalition for Human Needs for the national church and the late Lois Clark served on the Presiding Bishop's Fund for World Relief as well as with Women's Ministry.

Clark summarized the spirit of commitment and determination of Oklahoma Indian church people in her book, David Pendleton Oakerhater: God's Warrior, in which she wrote of Bishop Brooke's comment that the Cheyenne deacon was the ". . . remnant of the first attempt of our Church to do work among the Indians." She wrote:

> What the Bishop left unsaid was that the Church hierarchy had abandoned its work among (Oklahoma) Indians, but Oakerhater had not.

Celebration of Oakerhater feast days

The first feast day of David Pendleton Oakerhater — September 1, 1986 — was commemorated at the National Cathedral, Washington, D.C., with the bishop of Washington, John Thomas Walker, as celebrant. Preaching was Wantland. Lawrence Hart, a traditional chief of the Cheyenne nation as well as a relative of the deacon and a Mennonite minister, stood in the great cathedral attired in traditional Cheyenne clothing and read the gospel in the Cheyenne language. Other participants in the celebration were the Reverend George Smith (Ojibwa) of Minnesota, first chairperson of the National Committee on Indian Work (1969); Robert Two Bulls of South Dakota, first Native American intern at the National Cathedral; and these readers, all Native-born Oklahomans: the Reverend Barnett Jackson (Cherokee), Owanah Anderson (Choctaw), and Tim Tall Chief (Osage). Representatives of the Oakerhater family included a granddaughter, Elizabeth White Shield, and Dr. Henrietta Whiteman, then director of Indian education for the Bureau of Indian Affairs.

In 1987, Oklahomans observed the second feast day of Oakerhater with honor dances, traditional feasts, and broad participation by kinspeople at Roman Nose State Park. Nearby, the deacon saint had ministered among his Cheyenne people for 50 years. An open air early morning Eucharist was celebrated beneath tall trees at the pow-wow grounds with the bishop of Oklahoma, Gerald McAllister, as celebrant, and sermon by traditional Cheyenne Chief Lawrence Hart. Across America, there were special observances to celebrate the life and ministry of Oakerhater. The synod of Province of the Pacific paid special recognition at its opening Eucharist. In the Diocese of Central New York, communicants from the Onondaga Reservation took lead roles at Grace Church in Syracuse, where Oakerhater had been ordained 106 years before. In New Mexico, a special service was held at the cathedral of the Diocese of Rio Grande, led by members of the Albuquerque urban Indian congregation.

Wantland, the second American Indian to be consecrated bishop in the Episcopal Church, and who was named by Browning to head the Primate's Blue Ribbon Task Force of American Indian Affairs, concluded his sermon at the celebration of the first feast day,

> *...On August 31, 1931, Oakerhater died as he had lived, with full faith and trust in his captain, the Lord Jesus Christ. A busy non-Indian Church soon forgot the work of this saintly man. More than 30 years passed. But in the early 1960s, a family of Episcopalians moved to Watonga, Oklahoma, and finding no Episcopal community there, with cooperation of a nearby priest, placed a newspaper advertisement inviting all persons interested in the Episcopal Church to attend a meeting on a Sunday afternoon at the home of the new family.*

> *At the appointed date and time, over 30 loyal Cheyenne Indians appeared. These Churchmen had been nurtured in the Episcopal Church by David Oakerhater, and after his death by the Lay Readers that he had trained. After half a century, the Whirlwind Mission of the Holy Family emerged from the underground, and is again a mission of the Diocese of Oklahoma, and a living memorial to David Pendleton Oakerhater.*

The Episcopal Church in Navajoland

It was the women, carrying dispensary kits and school books, who first brought Episcopal witness to Navajoland, an immense land of high plateaus, deep and abrupt canyons, and fierce red rocks. The Navajo nation, the largest American Indian reservation, spills across parts of three states and is approximately the size of West Virginia. Home to approximately 180,000 of the tribe, Navajoland is at once a land of intense beauty and formidable isolation. It lacks adequate water, roads, and employment opportunities, and an estimated one-third of all Navajos come from non-English speaking homes.

Episcopal mission among the Navajo has centered in three pockets of the vast land. The New Mexico region, centered at Farmington, has four congregations; the Utah region, centered at Bluff, has three congregations and several house churches; the Southeast (Arizona) region, centered at Fort Defiance, eight miles from the Window Rock tribal headquarters, has four congregations and several house churches.

Beginning in the 1890s, a hardy throng of eastern women — medical missionaries and school teachers — left hearth and home in snug New England villages to toil in this distant arid land, ministering first to the physical ills of a nomadic desert people who called themselves Dine' (the people). The Spanish padres almost 300 years previously had introduced Christianity, often under duress, to the Pueblo neighbors of the Navajo. However, when the Episcopal medical missionaries arrived, the Dine' yet firmly held on to old beliefs centered on sacred mountains and monsters, all-powerful medicine men, myths and mysteries acted out in ceremony. The ladies from the east, products of the Victorian age, had scant capacity to fathom the soul of the Navajo.

Fort Defiance: Good Shepherd Mission

Episcopal mission in Navajoland had its beginnings in 1893 in faraway, cool, tree-covered Westchester county, New York when the Woman's Auxiliary of the county decided to help start drastically needed medical work on the Navajo Reservation.

When Eliza W. Thackara, who led the vanguard of Episcopal medical missionaries, in 1894 started building her hospital, primarily funded by the Westchester group, at Fort Defiance, the Navajo had been released only a short generation previously from internment at Bosque Redondo, 300 miles away in Mexico. Memories were still fresh in the minds of many who first came to Miss Thackara's hospital of the travail of the "hwelte" — the Long Walk — of 1864. Elders could remember the cherished peach orchards in Canyon de Chelly, destroyed by Kit Carson and his troops as they ruthlessly starved the Navajos toward surrender in a callous scorched earth tactic which saw eradication of fields, orchards, sheep, cattle, goats and horses of the Dine'. Seven thousand Navajo were rounded up from the mesas and mountains, held at Fort Defiance, then herded eastward to Fort Sumner and dumped for four years on a 40-square-mile barren area along the Pecos River.

At last, in 1868 the U. S. government, overwhelmed with the urgency of reconstruction following the Civil War, recognized its folly in attempting to transform the captive Navajo into skilled and schooled farmers and stockmen. More pressing was the reality that $1 million had been drained from federal coffers to care for the Navajo in the first 18 months of their Bosque Redondo captivity. Unscrupulous government agents siphoned two-thirds of the Navajo appropriation as graft before it ever reached the Indians. Propelled by exasperation, and in exchange for a promise of peace, the government made a treaty with the Navajos, signed June 1, 1868. On June 18, the Navajos headed westward toward the sacred mountains and vast empty spaces of the high desert plateau of the country they had claimed as home for around 500 years, drifting in some time in the 1200s — say the anthropologists — after somewhere in time separating from the distant Athabascans of Alaska. The difficult Athabascan and Navajo languages are still alike.

The treaty of 1868 allotted the Navajo a long, narrow rectangle of three and one-half million acres straddling the boarder between Arizona and New Mexico, leaving space of equal size to the west for the Hopi. No less than 15 federal ordinances and executive orders, between 1878 and 1934, expanded the Navajo Reservation, often overlapping previously assigned lands of other tribes, including the Hopi. In the Navajo resettlement, Fort Defiance became a center for distribution of food rations, seeds, tools and the sturdy little Spanish "churros" sheep — two animals for every man, woman and child. The government spent $30,000 to replace the sheep Kit Carson had killed. The first desperate decade after resettlement was a hard time for the Navajo; starvation was ever threatening. The over-confident lawmakers in Washington who thought the Navajo would promptly become settled farmers and stockmen, and thus, self-sufficient, never saw the soil of the reservation nor heard of its unseasonable frosts and droughts. Rations, meager and insufficient, continued. But it was out of this period that grew the famous Navajo weaving and silverwork, both crafted as items for trade.

The Navajo fell to the Presbyterians in the Grant peace policy apportionment and in 1869 they sent a young eastern lady, Charity Gaston, to start a school at Fort Defiance. When she arrived in her white shirtwaist and long black skirt, she found several hundred Navajo families gathered around the old fort, living in dugouts awaiting rations, seeds and tools. From lack of interest, the school failed and soon Miss Gaston married a local missionary and departed with him to work among the more "civilized" Pueblos. Various Presbyterian teachers came and went; pupils sporadically appeared and shortly departed. In 1880 the government built a boarding school for the Presbyterians at Fort Defiance. It was described as a dark and dreary, musty, adobe dungeon, and the expected 60 pupils failed to appear. The missionaries gave no weight to the cultural custom, wherein the Navajo lived from birth to death in a warm circle of family and clan mates.

By 1887 the federal government declared compulsory education for Indian children and government agents drove about in their buckboards collecting Navajo children, delivering them to Fort Defiance and thence dispatching the terrified children to schools from the reservation.

Such was the background of the land and people to which came Eliza Thackara, the well-educated daughter of a Florida priest. In the early 1890s she had visited military friends at Fort Defiance, and was distressed by the total lack of medical care for a people who suffered from epidemics, such as measles, brought by the white man. There was no treatment for tuberculosis nor trachoma, which caused blindness. Backed by John M. Kendrick, bishop of the Missionary District of Arizona and New Mexico, and by friends, Miss Thackara set out to build the first hospital on the vast Navajo reservation, "almost laying the stones herself."

The Episcopal hospital of the Good Shepherd at Fort Defiance opened in

1897 and Miss Thackara, whom the Navajo gave the name Woman Who Laughs, ran the hospital for 25 years. In the early years she found few Navajo availing themselves of the facility. Sick Navajos were appalled by the impersonal loneliness of hospital life; they were used to the tender solicitude of a whole family, and by the "sing" which, according to Navajo beliefs, brought the ill into direct communion with the spirits. Too, once a death had occurred in any building, the Navajo believed, it should at once be burned. Miss Thackara did not burn her new hospital building when a death occurred and, assumed certain of the Navajos, the building was surely contaminated by evil. In the Navajo ethos, a corpse lost all identity as kin, friend or clan mate, and became, instead, a source of supernatural contagion. In the early years only the dying were dispatched to Good Shepherd. Eventually, the hospital services were accepted, and by 1912 when the government built a hospital at the old fort, the Episcopal institution switched to a specialization in eye diseases.

While Miss Thackara toiled at Fort Defiance, other women in the east set out raising funds for the Navajo mission. Foremost among them continued to be the Westchester Woman's Auxiliary, led by Cornelia Jay and Fanny Schuyler. The original Chapel of the Good Shepherd, consecrated in 1911, was built as a memorial to Miss Jay. Little by little, new buildings were added and old ones enlarged on the 40-acre plot deeded by the Navajos. Many of the old buildings are today still in use for the delivery of community social and economic development programs.

In 1915 Anne E. Cady, who had been a missionary nurse in Alaska, came to Good Shepherd. She eventually succeeded Miss Thackara as superintendent, and propagated growth of the Navajo work until her retirement a quarter of a century later. Miss Cady started a field work program which Good Shepherd has continued. Outstation chapels were added — St. Anne's Chapel at Sawmill, 14 miles to the north; St. Luke's at Navajo, New Mexico; St. Mark's at Coal Mine, eight miles to the east.

As the government assumed greater responsibility for health care, the Good Shepherd Mission served as an orphanage, as a boarding school and later as a dormitory for reservation students in public and government schools. From the earliest days children lived at Good Shepherd mission. First they came as trachoma patients; gradually they appeared as orphan children. Among them was Thomas Atkinson, brought up from babyhood by Miss Thackara. The Navajo youth later studied at the Presbyterians' Cook Bible School in Phoenix and joined the Presbyterian Church. However, he returned to work at the Episcopal mission and was in time appointed as the first Navajo catechist. His early death in 1924 from tuberculosis was a major loss.

Another former student at Good Shepherd was Howard McKinley, described by Rosalie C. Tolman of the Executive Board for Woman's Auxiliary in a 1931 issue of *Spirit of Missions* as having come to the mission at age seven: "Despite his partial blindness from trachoma, he is the first Navajo Indian to have graduated from the University of New Mexico and has 30 hours toward his Master's Degree. To the boys at the mission he serves as a pattern to be followed." McKinley survives and on occasion visits Good Shepherd Church.

Janet Waring, vice president for Woman's Auxiliary for the Diocese of New York, in 1931 wrote an article for Spirit of Missions in which she described a visit to Good Shepherd Mission. She told of attempting in a rainstorm to reach the mission by automobile, which had to be abandoned when they reached a flooded arroyo:

> *The only habitation in which we could take refuge from the sudden and unexpected downpour was the hogan of Hosteen Nez, a full-blooded Navajo who in years gone by had worked for the founder of our mission, Miss Thackara. We found the family gathered in the one-room hogan, a low dome-like dwelling built of wattles and clay, with a door and a place for the smoke of fire to escape but no windows and with dirt floor. Furniture there was not, beds there were not, many sheep skins with an occasional Pendleton blanket indicated the sleeping places.*
>
> *After an hour the rain stopped. Then Hosteen harnessed the horses to the big lumber wagon, put boards across for seats. He and his sons waded in deep water above their waists, testing the river bottom, then by forcing the horses through the stream, we made a triumphal passage through the angry waters.*
>
> *Now we were in sight of the mission and of the belfry tower of the little Chapel of the Good Shepherd. The sun was pushing through heavy clouds and there lay before us a scene as pastoral as any ever seen by the shepherds of Palestine. Before us over a wide stretch of valley were flocks of beautiful white sheep, three to four hundred, enfolded and watched by Navajo women. The Navajo women own and are the custodians of the sheep.*
>
> *Picturesque are the clothes of the women. . . silver buttons on their tight-fitting waists, and often a silver necklace of remarkable workmanship, as well as bright beads. Their skirts, of which they wear four to eight, are very full and each has a flounce measuring from 12 to 15 yards around. Their long black hair is done in a sort of "bob-knot" at the back of the neck and all wound 'round with a woolen string.*
>
> *We had arrived at the gateway, surmounted by its stone cross. To the left was the chapel built in memory of Miss Cornelia Jay. Its bell rings out over the silent desert for daily services. The forty acres*

on which the school stands was deeded to the Church by the Nava-
jos themselves.

It was, I learned, the season for sheep dipping, and Fort Defi-
ance is one of the chief government dips. There are strict regula-
tions obliging the Navajos to bring their flocks here once a year,
to be driven through the long deep trough of medicated bath.

Later from my bedroom window in the mission, I looked out on
a picturesqe encampment spread over the wide country, the Navajo
families gathered around their camp fires, sheep skins drying on the
sand. A flicker of twenty or more camp fires made an unforgettable
picture.

By 1954 the growth of the congregation and the near collapse of the original chapel at the mission made the building of the present Chapel of the Good
Shepherd a necessity. Given in memory of Elisabeth H. Davis by her husband, Arthur Vining Davis, the chapel is strikingly designed to harmonize
with the land and people; Navajo craftsmanship and symbolism are represented
in its vessels and furnishing. *The Trail Ahead,* published in 1955 by the National Council of the Episcopal Church, describes the consecration of the new
chapel:

On Sunday, July 7, 1955, four hundred Navajos and two hundred
non-Indians came together at the Mission of the Good Shepherd,
to participate in the dedication of a new chapel. A non-Navajo-
speaking Indian clergyman preached; his words were interpreted by
a Navajo. After the service there was a procession to the new clergy
house which too was dedicated. In the traditional Navajo manner
feasting followed, and in the background there was Navajo music
by Navajo musicians. The service was one the Navajos themselves
had requested as the proper way to launch the use of the new mis-
sion buildings.

New Mexico: San Juan Mission

To the New Mexico region of present-day Navajoland Area Mission came
another woman of faith, patience and vision. She helped to establish San Juan
Mission, named for the San Juan River which flows nearby and located near
Farmington, New Mexico, only a stone's throw from the eastern boundary
of the vast reservation. This woman was Mattie C. Peters, who came in 1917
to establish the small 20-bed hospital which provided the only medical care
for the entire eastern sweep of the reservation. In a 1925 issue of *Spirit of
Missions,* she wrote:

It was my privilege to be the first one sent by the Church to this far-away corner of the Navajo country to establish, first of all, a dispensary work and to open a house by the side of the trail, which for seven years was a Mission of hope and help to hundreds of Indians living on the large Reservation. I occupied and opened the little house in January 1917 and for 15 months I carried on without an associate worker. In time there came, one by one, UTO workers, but at no time did the staff consist of more than two, yet the work went on in the Mission House, and some field work was done on the Reservation.

Our several years experiences with epidemics, trachoma, tuberculosis and other diseases, revealed more and more the crying need of a hospital, and gradually my lovely dream of a home and school for some of the 1,500 neglected children of the Reservation faded, giving way to a vision of an institution for the sick of all ages.

After six years of hoping and planning, through gifts of United Thank Offering and many friends, the Mary E. Hart Memorial Hospital and Chapel stand today not far from the Reservation line. Opening of the hospital was not as I had hoped. My own plan to include some formality and ceremony was sidetracked, and the hospital was opened with neither doctor nor nurse in charge. . .only untrained help. Before we could get the house into any kind of order, we were called upon to open the wards to sick folks.

An epidemic of measles was raging out on the Reservation and many children, and even men and women, had already died for want of medical help. During the remainder of December we cared for patients in the wards and visited and cared for stricken Indians in nearby camps. Just three days before Christmas, a young girl passed away. She was the fifth child of one family to die within two weeks. Her death cast a shadow over our preparations for Christmas festivities. But, by Christmas morning everything was in readiness. We entertained our Indian guests, 150 strong. We did not attempt a full service, but the Christmas story was told through an interpreter. It was a touching sight to see those pagan Indians — as many as could be crowded into the chapel — on their knees while the simple prayers were said.

Miss Peters was later assisted at the San Juan Mission by Miss Emily Ireland, a trained nurse, who came into the work with experience and missionary zeal. Because of ill health, Miss Peters had to resign in 1924. During seven years, however, she had brought Navajo mission significantly forward, leaving two field outstations, both operated by women. St. Luke's-in-the-Desert, at Carson's Trading Post, was 28 miles out in the reservation, and work at Aneth, Utah, was 100 miles north and west of San Juan. St. Luke's is still active but the Aneth work ceased.

Jane Turnbull, another registered nurse, came as a UTO worker to the San Juan hospital in 1926, intending to stay one year. She remained among the Navajo for 58 years, until her death in 1984. Miss Turnbull at times was the only medical help to the Navajos; she delivered many Navajo babies into the world. A survivor at her death was her adopted Navajo daughter.

Navajo volunteers, since the early days, assisted with the hospital. Katherine Jim, among the first Navajo volunteers, and her husband, George Jim, were the last survivors of the crew which laid the stones for the hospital building. Family members of Mr. and Mrs. Jim are among today's leaders in the Episcopal community in the New Mexico district of Navajoland; a granddaughter, Rosella Jim, serves on the national church's Standing Commission on Structure.

The old hospital, which closed in 1959, now houses offices for the Episcopal Church in Navajoland. Up a stony pathway from the old hospital is All Saints' Church, fittingly decorated with fine hand-woven Navajo rugs, colorful banners and altar hangings, and an arrestingly rustic stylized crucifix, crafted by Victoria John, a parishioner and another granddaughter of Mr. and Mrs. Jim. In addition to the All Saints' congregation, today's New Mexico region has St. Michael's congregation at Fruitland and St. Augustine's at Shiprock.

Navajo mission in the Utah Strip

Laura M. Parmelee, accompanied by another woman identified only as Miss Ross, in 1923 began the Aneth work. Miss Parmelee described the outstations:

> *On the San Juan River, 25 miles east of the little settlement of Bluff, Utah, entirely Mormon. I do not know of one Christian Navajo living here. During the year, I treated 928 dispensary cases. All told, there have been over 1,400 Navajo visitors.*
>
> *In the 14 months we have been here, we have had but five opportunities for the Holy Communion. Will those of you who have the privilege of kneeling at a real altar please remember this work and the two workers?*

Miss Parmelee's work in the Utah "strip" would be dramatically revived 20 years later with the arrival of the Reverend Harold Baxter Liebler, who is said to have baptized 10,000 Navajos.

It was in the summer of 1942 that the middle-aged Liebler rode horseback alone along the sheer sandstone cliffs that parallel the San Juan River in southeastern Utah. He was looking for a place to establish a mission among the Navajo. He found a place called Hydrum's Field, near the hamlet of Bluff, where fresh water dripped from a slit in the otherwise impregnable and barren sandstone wall. His first mass was said on St. Christopher's Day, and since St. Christopher is the patron saint of those who travel, the mission had its name. Here Liebler would remain for 23 years.

The Brooklyn-born, Columbia University-educated priest has been ordained in 1914 and had served St. Savior's Church in Old Greenwich, Connecticut, for 25 years. Since seminary days at Nashotah House, he had held an ardent interest in Indian cultures which he knew well and respected, and he deplored the efforts of missionaries to destroy all that remained of the beauty of Indian life rather than enriching it with the truth and grace of the gospel. He had made several trips into Navajoland, and spent months in study of the difficult Navajo language with its strange sounds, high and low tones and nasalized vowels. Starting with $1,000 in donated funds, six volunteers and a hired Navajo, a temporary mission house was built from the red sandstone of the southeastern Utah desert. Gradually, the small band erected a church building and mission house, a school, and a 12-bed clinic and other facilities and improvements.

In the early months at the mission Liebler established himself with the Navajo Indians as a man with strong medicine. "I needed an idea to put over the crucifixion, and decided to use the sand painting," he said. Unwittingly, he utilized certain symbols in the sand painting that the Navajo use in rain-making ceremonies. That night a heavy downpour not only drenched the area, but flooded out part of the mission. One of his converts, awed by the storm, said to the priest, "Father, that was some rain you made yesterday."

As the years passed, Liebler's congregation grew until it covered much of the Utah part of the Navajo Reservation. In 1966, at age 77, Liebler, along with three members of the mission staff, which then numbered around 20, retired to the Monument Valley area, approximately 60 miles to the southeast, to build the little hogan Church of St. Mary's-of-the-Moonlight. After 42 years of living among the Navajo, Harold Liebler died in 1982, at 93, and was buried on the grounds of St. Christopher's mission.

St. Christopher's Chapel is architecturally remarkable. A tall wooden cone, it prompts an impression of a plains Indian tepee. For lack of funds the building was never completed; the congregation meets in a remodeled school building. Eight other buildings, some dating back to Liebler's era, remain in the Episcopal compound two miles east of Bluff. Also remaining nearby is a swinging bridge which Navajo children formerly used to cross the sometimes turbulent San Juan River to attend Liebler's school.

Steven Tsosie Plummer, the first Navajo ordained to the priesthood, became resident priest for St. Christopher's in 1983, also serving St. Mary's-of-the-Moonlight, and St. John the Baptizer at Montezuma Creek, adjacent to Aneth. Born in 1944 at Coal Mine, New Mexico, Plummer was a ninth-grade drop-out. He later returned to Albuquerque Indian School, took courses at Cook Christian Training Sₗ hool, Tempe, Arizona; at Phoenix Junior College, and in 1975 after two years' study was granted a certificate from Church Divinity School of the Pacific. He was ordained to the diaconate in 1975 and to the priesthood in 1976.

Joseph M. Harte, retired bishop of Arizona, tells a wonderful story about his ordaining Plummer. The bishop asked his Navajo flock where they wanted their first Episcopal clergyman ordained and was informed the event should take place in Canyon de Chelly, a magnificently colored and awe-inspiring chasm in the heart of the Navajo nation. The bishop asked why at this distant place. "It is a holy place," replied the Navajo. The bishop asked why the Navajo specifically identified Canyon de Chelly as a holy place. The Navajo, drawing from their traditional creation story responded, "Because Spider Woman lives there."

St. Luke's-in-the-Desert

In 1924 Lena Wilcox apparently went alone out into the reservation, near Carson's Trading Post, to bring the gospel to the Navajo. She set up a dispensary and began informally to teach. A writer for *Spirit of Missions* 60 years ago explained that the Navajo people refer to themselves as Dine', translating as "the people." The writer termed Miss Wilcox's work as an intelligent venture, stating:

> Since "the people" are nomadic, following their sheep herds, they do not live in villages. The Church, in order to reach them at all, must go to where they do most resort, at a trading post.

By 1930, the owner of the trading post had given five acres on which was built the chapel, St. Luke's-in-the-Desert. Built of native stone, it had vigas (roof-beams) in the old Spanish fashion of the country, and the altar was inlaid with a panel of petrified wood. The candlesticks were hand-made from native pine, and the dossal was a Navajo rug.

Miss Wilcox described St. Luke's as the only religious, social or medical center in the entire district of about 5,000 square miles. She wrote, "The mission stands in almost the center of this vast tract of sand and sagebrush and there is probably not a Navajo in the entire district who has not at some time, in some way, felt the influence of its ministry."

After Miss Wilcox had lived and worked in the remote outstation for 15 years she wrote a reflective article for *Spirit of Missions* in a vein exceedingly uncommon to her era. She weighed characteristics of Navajo traditional religion and its quest for harmony, but faulted the "hold" the medicine man had over the people. She believed the deplorable disease rate and resulting human suffering justified on-going Episcopal mission. In 1937, she wrote:

Ho, ho, ho, ho.
Ee, hee, hee, hee, yah, hee yah.
Oh ho, ho, ho.
Ee, hee, hee, hee, yah, hee, yah.
Dolah, ah-nee, ee-ee-ee-ee-ee-ee.
Ee, oh, oh, hoh. Hee yah, hee yah.
Ee, yah, ee, oh.
Oh, ho, hee yah, ee, hee.

Chanted to the muffled cadence of rattles and the soft thud of moc-casined feet, the last song of the Navajo's nine day Night Chant, or Yabaichai ceremony, floats in through the desert night, bringing with it the spicy smell of burning sagebrush and the smoke of many fires. For nine nights the Navajos have been holding this great ceremony of healing and supplication to the gods; and now the last of the chants floats in as they conclude the ceremony with the chant to the blue-bird, just at sunrise on the last morning.

Across the arroyo in the opposite direction stands the rugged cross of St. Luke's-in-the-Desert, outlined against a sky of turquoise blue. On the one hand, the age-old religion of the Navajos, handed down for generations, their only means of expressing a religious life that is fundamental in the life of all Indians and the Navajos. On the other hand, the new and to the Navajo Indian, unproven religion of the white man. Just where to draw the line between the two, or how to lead from one to the other is a question every missionary in the Indi-an country must face.

Time and again we are asked, and at times I myself have almost wondered as I have watched the intricate making of a sand painting or listened to the reverent and impressive chanting of the medicine man, if it were not better to leave the Navajo to pursue undisturbed his own colorful rites and ceremonies.

Vision for the second century of Navajo ministry

Sanction to enable the Navajo to pursue their own direction within the framework of the Episcopal Church has been an issue for decades. The hierarchy of the church, as far back as the 1950s and as recently as the 1985 General Convention, has fretted over "what to do about the Navajos," often without consulting the Navajos. Thirty years ago it was recognized that

Episcopal mission with the largest of the country's Indian nations had to be unified, and that the separation of the church's missions into three dioceses (Arizona, Rio Grande, and Utah) was not in harmony with other Navajo tribal activities. In 1973 the House of Bishops rejected a proposal for a Navajo diocese but directed that a Navajo council be formed, and, thus, was born the Episcopal Church in Navajoland (ECN). In 1977 the House of Bishops voted to unify Navajo work into a single jurisdiction but the entity created — Navajoland Area Mission — is unique within the structure of the Episcopal Church. Its bishop is appointed, not elected; its General Convention deputies have no vote and are seated in a separate designated section. In fact, the character and configuration of the Navajo Area Mission more closely parallels the 19th century missionary jurisdiction of Niobrara — the nongeographical jurisdiction of the Sioux — than the 98 U. S. dioceses of the Episcopal Church of the late 1980s.

The historic Missionary District of Niobrara weathered 10 transitional years in its original configuration, and exactly a decade after formation of Navajoland Area Mission, the ECN Council studied, drafted, presented and adopted a proposal for a new status in the church. The plan will be offerred to the 1988 General Convention.

Two factor motivated the 1987 ECN proposal. First the 1985 General Convention called for a study of the mission status of Navajoland within the triennium. Second, the interim and part-time bishop had disclosed plans to resign after the 1988 convention.

In the summer of 1987 the eight Navaho women on the ECN Council stepped forward to articulate a vision of the Episcopal Church in Navajoland. Nineteenth-century white women brought the Episcopal mission to the Navajo; 20th century Navajo women pondered pathways toward full partnership in the Episcopal Church in the 21st century. The ECN Council, representing 2,900 Episcopal-baptized Navajos, over a six-month period had scrutinized alternatives. Council members smarted over the fact their deputies had no vote; they felt an urgency about the pending vacancy in the episcopacy. The council, along with 300 others, came to the old San Juan mission for the 12th annual Navajo Convocation in June, 1987, and adopted a "second decade" plan. The National Committee on Indian Work, citing the proposal as a step to empowerment, endorsed it.

The proposal recommends that Navajoland remain an area mission but that it have sanction to make a significant step toward autonomy through nominating to the House of Bishops its choice for bishop, and establishing a partnership relation with a neighboring diocese for mutual support and resource sharing. The proposal looks toward further expanded mission by offering the Navajoland bishop and people in a supportive role to other Native American work of the western dioceses and provinces. Discussion at the convocation raised up a conviction that in the second century of ministry among the Navajo the church must sanction Navajo partnership in the broader church and offer potential for indigenous empowerment and autonomy.

The decade 1977 to 1987 was a growth period in Navajoland. Canonical organization absorbed attention in the early years; Otis Charles, then of Utah, was bishop-in-charge. In 1979 Frederick Putnam, former suffragan bishop of Oklahoma, was appointed full-time resident bishop, serving through 1982. In 1983 Wes Frensdorff, then of Nevada, was appointed interim bishop on a quarter-time basis. With consistent integrity, Frensdorff has been witness to self-determination, shepherding the Council of ECN toward empowerment in church polity — a consummate reversal from early missionizing mentality which not only perpetuated paternalism but created dependence.

Perhaps the most significant growth factor has been the once-isolated Navajo assuming new responsibilities in the life of the church. In 1985 the first Navajo priest, Fr. Plummer, became "adah sedahi," presiding elder. As such he presided — and provided bilingual translation — at the ECN Council jointly with Frensdorff, who in 1985 became assistant bishop of Arizona. The decade saw Buddy Arthur emerge as a postulant for holy orders, two women appointed to national church commissions, strong new emphasis on youth work, and a dozen adults come forward to participate in summer seminars taught by professors from Seabury-Western Theological Seminary.

When the 1985 General Convention called for a review of the status and concept of the Navajoland Area Ministry, it directed that the study be conducted by the Standing Commission on Structure. The Presiding Bishop appointed to that commission a strong young Navajo woman, Rosella Jim, who has carried well the message of her Navajo constituency. Mrs. Jim stood before the Episcopal World Missions Conference in the summer of 1986 at Sewanee, Tennessee, and voiced an affirmation of her people when she said, "We thank you for bringing us the gospel. We must carry on now ourselves."

On trial is a concept widely-promoted by top-level church leadership in the last decade of "indigenization of indigenous ministry," proposed a century ago by the Anglican missionary to China, Roland Allen. Sitting as jury is the 1988 General Convention of the Episcopal Church. At question is whether the Navajo will, within the framework of the Episcopal Church, be enabled to pursue their own direction.

San Juan Indian Hospital at Farmington, N.M.

Chapter 7

Episcopal work in the mountains and desert

The Episcopal Church brought the gospel in the last decades of the 19th century to the Shoshone, Arapaho, Ute, Paiute and Bannock tribes, who were by then isolated on reservations in pockets among the mountains and desert of the immense inland region of the west. Work was begun with zeal and promise. On two of the reservations, acceptance of the white man's religion came with extraordinary swiftness; 90 per cent of the Utes and almost all the Pyramid Lake Paiutes were once confirmed Episcopalians. By the mid-1980s, however, Episcopal ministry in the inland west had seriously decreased. No new ministry had begun in generations. In the dioceses of Nevada, Idaho, Utah and Wyoming, areas of promise 100 years ago, only five Indian congregations were holding regular worship services.

A reawakening began in the summer of 1987. After almost a decade, a congregation on the Uintah Reservation reactivated regular weekly services. A diocese which had never had Indian work — Montana — was organizing new Native American outreach. Even more far-reaching, a new mutual support coalition was organized that summer. Two dozen representatives, predominantly Indian from the dioceses of Idaho, Montana, Utah and Wyoming convened at historic Wind River Reservation in Wyoming and formed Mountains and Desert Regional American Indian Ministry. A fifth diocese, Nevada, was invited to link with the new coalition. Isolation from each other and isolation from diocesan, provincial and national church structures had been a common concern expressed by communicants of five Indian congregations of the region, an area in the late 1980s noted for a climate of racism relating to American Indians. A message sent to the national church from the new coalition was a petition for "a freedom from worry that the Episcopal Church will abandon us."

Wind River Reservation, Wyoming

It was seemly that the new coalition was launched on the Wind River Reservation where Episcopal mission among the tribes of the mountains and desert began. Old missionary journals have told highly romanticized tales about the cast of characters instrumental in setting the Wind River mission afloat — John Roberts, Sherman Coolidge and Chief Washakie. Elders on Wind River Reservation, however, say many of these stories are more legend that truth. Nonetheless, Episcopal work did begin on the Wind River in 1883 and two congregations, St. David's on the Shoshone Reservation and St. Michael's on the Arapaho Reservation, have survived.

The Shoshone and Bannock on Wind River were parceled to the Episcopal

Church in the 1872 Grant peace agreement. The following year, George Randall, the first missionary bishop of Colorado, paid a visit to the reservation and conducted the first Episcopal services in a little log cabin. But due to the strain of the arduous journey and exposure to grim winter days, Randall contracted pneumonia and died.

A treaty had been made with the Shoshone and Bannock Indians in 1868 which reserved for these tribes a million-and-a-half acre tract in a great valley along the Wind River of Wyoming. The venerable old Chief Washakie, around whom many mission stories are woven, signed the treaty on behalf of the Shoshone, who claimed to have occupied the lush valley since the 1700s. The Bannocks did not long remain on the Wind River Reservation but returned to their traditional homelands in Idaho.

Meanwhile, the Arapaho Indians, of an entirely different linguistic stock from the Shoshone, after having been jostled from place to place by the federal government, appeared on Wind River in the cold winter of 1876. Federal authorities asked Washakie to quarter the Arapaho until spring. The chief agreed; the Arapaho have been at Wind River ever since. Sixty years went by before the federal government made any cash settlement to the Shoshone for the eastern part of the reservation occupied by the Arapaho. From the beginning, the two tribes remained aloof from each other and certain tensions still surface between these neighbors on adjoining reservations. And, almost from the beginning, the Episcopal Church has maintained distinctly separate mission with the Shoshone and the Arapaho.

Shoshone mission

In 1883 a young Welshman, filled with missionary zeal, departed the green meadows of Britain to establish the Church on Wind River Reservation. His name was John Roberts and he would remain on Wind River for 66 years. Roberts had been ordained in the cathedral in Lichfield by the great apostle to New Zealand, Bishop Selwyn. The old Episcopal periodical, *Spirit of Missions* described young Roberts' arrival:

> *Wyoming at that time was virgin country; civilization had scarcely penetrated across the border, and the only means of travel beyond the terminus of the Union Pacific was the prairie schooner. It was February, 1883, and Wyoming was blanketed with the deepest snow in years, and Mr. Roberts was obliged to make the trip of 150 miles from Green River to Fort Washakie with the mail carrier. When they left Green River, it was 60 degrees below zero.*
> *It took eight days to make the trip. At one place along the road, a young woman passenger was so badly frostbitten that Mr. Roberts stayed up all night chopping wood to keep a fire going so that she*

might be warm. In spite of that, she died the next day. Another day the stage driver was frozen to death, and Mr. Roberts drove the horses to the next station, trusting their instincts to find the way.

Roberts at first found growth of his mission very slow but gradually he earned the respect of the tribesmen. During the first year he established a small school and enrolled 16, and by 1886 he had been engaged to superintend the government boarding school for 86 Indian children. Indian catechists and lay helpers, unnamed in literature, were trained under tutelage of Roberts. With the help of the Shoshones, he translated parts of the Bible and The Book of Common Prayer. In 1899 Chief Washakie gave Roberts 160 acres to be used as the Shoshone Indian Mission School for Girls, which operated for many years.

There are fascinating stories in the old periodical, *Spirit of Missions,* about the late night conversion and baptism of the venerable Old Chief Washakie. Wind River descendants of Washakie, however, say the stories are not factual. Furthermore, Washakie's baptismal records reveal that he was baptized at age 100, only three years before his death. Whether the Washakie baptismal story is fact or fiction, it is sketched herein because it has become a legend:

One day Washakie's son went to the village, consumed too much alcohol, and in an ensuing fray with U.S. soldiers was killed. From his high mountain dwelling, Washakie sent word that in revenge he would come down the mountain the following day and kill every white man he met until he himself was killed. Then, Washakie went to bed.

Soon Washakie was awakened by someone seeking admittance to his lodge. It was the young priest, who said, "If you carry out this threat, the white men will kill you. You are the best chief your people have ever had, and they need you. You must not be killed. I am young and have few friends and will not be greatly missed. Therefore, take my life in exchange for that of your son."

Washakie, who reverently admired courage and bravery, could not take the life of the young missionary. What, he wanted to know, gave young Roberts such courage? The two men sat down to talk together, and at 3 a.m. Washakie was baptized. Chief Washakie, who governed his people for 70 years, lived to be 103. The Rev. Roberts officiated at the funeral of the old chief who was buried with full military honors.

Roberts also officiated a year after his arrival at the Wind River Reservation at the burial at the Shoshone cemetery of another figure around whom there is much mystery. Legend claims she was Sacajawea, one of the best-known Indian women of all time, who, in 1806 led the Lewis and Clark expedition across the Rocky Mountains to the Pacific Ocean. A question remains, and scholars disagree, as to whether this aged woman was, in fact, Sacajawea, lost for 50 years and discovered at death to have been quietly back among her Shoshone people on the Wind River Reservation. The woman buried at Wind River is identified in church records simply as "Baptiste's mother." Baptiste was, in fact, the name of the little boy called "Pomp" in the Lewis and Clark journals and it is Baptiste who is depicted straddling the back of the young Sacajawea in the many statues sprinkled across the country. Only God knows who actually lies buried at the Shoshone cemetery. However, in the great valley between the Shining Mountains, the Wind River Range and the Owl Creek Mountains, a substantial gray-granite column attests:

SACAJAWEA
DIED APRIL 9, 1884
A GUIDE WITH THE LEWIS AND CLARK EXPEDITION
1805-1806
IDENTIFIED, 1907, BY REV. J. ROBERTS
WHO OFFICIATED AT HER BURIAL

Arapaho mission and the first Arapaho priest

Episcopal work among the Arapaho was begun by an Arapaho, the first of his tribe ordained to the priesthood. He was Sherman Coolidge, who for 25 years served the northern Arapaho mission at Wind River, helped at intervals at the southern Cheyenne-Arapaho mission of David Pendleton Oakerhater in Oklahoma, and as an old man is glimpsed in the role of honorary canon of St. John's Cathedral in Denver.

Conflicting accounts of the events which shaped the life of the Arapaho priest appeared in old missionary journals, the disparity likely a result of perspective. Around 1869 Desche-Wash-Ah, a young Arapaho boy, was captured — whether by the Shoshone or the military remains at question — and brought to a military garrison near Lander, Wyoming. He was adopted by Captain and Mrs. Charles A. Coolidge, who changed his name to Sherman Coolidge.

Conflict in the Indian/white perspective is clearly demonstrated in the attitude relating to the battle of Little Big Horn, shown in this 1931 article in *Spirit of Missions:*

> *In 1876 Sherman was tall and strong for his 14 years, and except for the garb of civilization, a typical young warrior of the Arapahos. For seven months in 1877 [every Indian knows that the reference here to 1877 to be in error; Little Big Horn battle was fought June 25, 1876], he campaigned with Captain Coolidge against a powerful and deadly foe, the Sioux, the Cheyennes and the Arapahos. There were many skirmishes during the spring and summer of*

that year but the principal conflict was that of the Little Big Horn. Captain Coolidge and his adopted son were not in this historic battle, being at the time about 80 miles away, but as soon as the news of the battle was brought by the couriers, General Terry ordered a forced march to help Custer. Artillery, infantry, cavalry, and ammunition were taken, but reached the scene too late.

Young Sherman decided that he wanted to be a minister. Old journals say, "at first the Coolidges opposed their foster son's choice of a profession on grounds that he was not suited to such a calling." In 1877, however, Sherman entered Shattuck Episcopal Military School in Faribault, Minnesota. Bishop Whipple, in his autobiography, tells of the young student who excelled in his school work. He came to the bishop one day and said, "Bishop, I suppose I am the only Arapaho who has become a Christian, and I should like to become a missionary to my people." Whipple entered Coolidge in Seabury Divinity School, where he was an excellent student, and ordained him to the diaconate in 1884. Whipple's autobiography also says:

Upon his arrival at Wind River an Indian woman, led by a mother's instinct, ran toward him crying, "You are my son!" And, so it proved. He afterward had the privilege of leading the heathen mother to the Savior.

He was ordained priest by John F. Spalding, bishop of Colorado, in 1885. At Wind River, Fr. Roberts' primary duty was to the Shoshone. Work among the Arapaho was begun in earnest with return of Coolidge to his home reservation. A brief reference in an undated Episcopal publication, *On the Trail to Tomorrow,* says Michael Whitehawk translated St. Luke's gospel into Arapaho and that St. Michael's Mission was named in his honor.

In 1913 property was acquired to establish an Arapaho mission and the Arapaho called it "Hethadee," meaning "good." The word was eventually anglicized into "Ethete," and became the name for the mission's post office.

In 1914 St. Michael's Mission was established. The design of the complex was in the form of a circle, as would be an Indian camp. The mission became noted as an experiment in aiding the Indian to make a transition. A notable quote from a 1918 issue of *Spirit of Missions* bespeaks, perhaps unwittingly, of a certain integrity:

Saint Michael's Mission to the Arapahos does not aim at making a white man out of the Indian. It is a mission school situated on the Reservation on which the Indians are obliged to live. Those who are educated under the eyes of their elders are not ostracized when the time of their home-going arrives.

Roberts appears to have earned an unparalleled confidence among the Arapaho people. A 1928 issue of *Spirit of Missions* says:

> *Many years ago, during an Indian uprising, Mr. Roberts was made custodian of the sacred pipe of the Arapahos. This pipe is the most sacred possession of the Indians, and very few white men have been permitted even to see it.*

One senses that perhaps the early Wind River mission, under the Welsh and the Arapaho priests, was generations ahead of the rest of the church in honoring the integrity of native traditions and cultural values.

The boarding school served as the cornerstone for the Wind River mission. Among the Shoshone there was the school for girls and among the Arapaho the esteemed St. Michael's. Though the schools closed decades ago, work continues among the estimated 1,900 baptized Episcopalians of the Wind River Reservation. The smaller Shoshone congregation worships at St. David's, near Fort Washakie. The Arapaho congregation worships at Our Father's House in the St. Michael's compound, which houses a variety of community social and educational programs. A full-time, non-Indian priest serves the Arapaho congregation, and Stan VerStraten and his wife, Judy, are central to a variety of community outreach programs from restoring the splendid old mission complex to guiding growth of a children's center.

Significant ecumenical activity is found at Wind River. The annual July pow-wow concludes with an open-air eucharistic celebration, opening with traditional Arapaho ceremonies, and featuring the Episcopal priest and the Roman Catholic priest as concelebrants.

Idaho: 100 years at Fort Hall

The first seminary-educated ordained woman priest to serve an Indian congregation came in 1985 to the Church of the Good Shepherd at Fort Hall, Idaho. It was at this historic fort, established in the early 1800s to protect white immigrants on the Oregon Trail as well as to keep a watchful eye on the Shoshone and Bannock tribes, that the first Episcopal services were held in the present Diocese of Idaho. The year was 1834. During the century and a half from then until the arrival of the Rev. Joan LaLiberte, a number of women had assiduously ministered among the Native peoples of Fort Hall Reservation and had, in fact, been pace-setters for ecumenical collegiality.

Under terms of the Grant Peace Policy, the Episcopal Church agreed to assume religious oversight for the Shoshone and Bannock tribes in Wyoming Territory, as well as for five Dakota agencies and a Ponca agency. Thus, technically, Bishop Hare of Niobrara had early jurisdiction over the Shoshone and Bannocks. His Dakota charges, however, consumed his total time and energy. Meanwhile, the Bannocks departed Wyoming and united with a separate band of Shoshone. In 1869 a half-million acre tract was reserved near Pocatello, Idaho, for the "Sho-Bans." Initially, operation of the government agency serving the Sho-Bans was passed among various denominations. First it was Methodist-Episcopal, then Presbyterian, in 1871 Roman Catholic, in 1873 back to the Methodists. By 1883 the Mormons appeared. At last, in 1889, the Episcopal Church came to Fort Hall to stay.

The women missionaries arrived in 1887 to establish a mission school. First to appear was Amelia J. Frost who was sent by an interdenominational Connecticut Indian Association. Two years later the Connecticut group approached James B. Funsten, missionary bishop of Idaho, to assume responsibility, and he accepted. Shortly thereafter Ella Stiles arrived and was teacher at the school for 10 years. Susan Garrett came in 1900 to develop more fully the program of the school, and in 1901 it is recorded that there were eight baptisms at Miss Garrett's station.

The school's program was standard for the era — agriculture studies for the boys, housekeeping training for the girls — with a fourth "R" in the curriculum for religious education. In 1908 the bishop acquired 160 acres to enlarge the farm program and until the 1930s, when the government began to operate reservation day schools, the Mission of the Good Shepherd molded the minds of the young Sho-Bans.

The building for the Church of the Good Shepherd was erected in the late 1800s, the present education facility around 1905. In 1984 the church building was deemed structurally unsafe, and was promptly condemned, padlocked, and a beam nailed across the front door. The 100-plus community of baptized Episcopalians continued regular worship services in the education building which had undergone extensive renovation through United Thank Offering funding.

At the same time that the bishop of Idaho, David Birney, was seeking money from the Episcopal Church to repair the Church of the Good Shepherd, the vestry and congregation were urgently voicing another priority. The senior warden, Lillian Vallely, said, "Sure we would like to see our church building repaired. It's a demoralizing symbol with a board nailed across the front door and makes a statement to the Reservation about the Episcopal Church. However, we do have a place to worship; we can use the education building. What we need most at Fort Hall is a resident priest to help us grow spiritually, to give us leadership in youth programs, to minister to our people." And, thus it was that Joan LaLiberte, through funding assistance from the National Committee on Indian Work, joined other women in ministry among the Shoshone-Bannock at Fort Hall, Idaho. Though the building had not been repaired by mid-1987, work on it was a self-help priority of the new Mountains and Desert regional coalition. The United Thank Offering in late summer of 1987 granted the project $22,000.

With LaLiberte came new initiatives in youth ministry and alcoholism programs. Traditional people had become more accepting of a woman in the role of priest, and steps had been taken toward reconciliation between Christians and people who practice the traditional religion.

Nevada and the Paiute plight

It was in 1895 that the Paiutes of Pyramid Lake were assigned to the Episcopal Church. Again, women came from distant places equipped with medical kits, school books, coping skills, and determination to share Christian compassion with the Native peoples of the desert. First to come to Pyramid Lake, in 1896, was Marian Taylor, supported by the Woman's Auxiliary of the Diocese of Western New York. She remained until her death in 1910. Her leadership and the leadership of women who followed her, including Deaconess Lucy N. Carter, earned early and broad response from the Paiutes, and within a quarter of a century almost all of the Pyramid Lake Paiutes had been baptized in the Episcopal Church.

In addition to Pyramid Lake, two other reservations, far removed from each other, were assigned to the Episcopal Church — Moapa and Fort McDermitt. Work was begun at Moapa in 1917 and at Fort McDermitt in 1932, and at one time there were two congregations at Pyramid Lake. Only St. Mary's at Nixon remains.

The church building of St. Mary's, erected in 1917, is a beautiful little structure seating approximately 150. Copperish-brown hues highlight the faces of the carved statues; Indian characteristics are evident in the figures of the stations of the cross; an olive skinned madonna looks down upon the Paiute people. Incongruous, however, is the old two-story white Cape Cod rectory, standing defiantly at the edge of the desert. A spacious parish hall was completed and used first for festivities of Christmas 1931.

The priest at St. Mary's, William Hannafin, has done much of his ministry among American Indians, including the Navajo. The bishop of Nevada, Stewart Zabriskie, consecrated in 1986, brought with him an unusually broad knowledge of and sensitivity for Native American issues, having served previously in the Diocese of Minnesota where native work has long been a focus. The concern of all church people of the diocese and the broader church is sorely needed by the troubled people of the Pyramid Lake Reservation.

Since first encounter with whites, the Pyramid Lake Paiutes have been forced to fight for survival of their lake, their subsistence and their life style. The turquoise blue, fan-shaped lake, 30 miles long and 11 miles at its widest, has been described as the most beautiful of all the desert lakes. It gained its name from a pyramid-shaped island which rises almost 300 feet from the water near the eastern shore. On the lake's shores since ancient times have lived the Cui-ui-Ticutta, now officially known as the Pyramid Lake Paiute.

These people subsisted primarily on the lake's fine fish, including the giant Lahontan cutthroat trout, a species found in no other part of the world. Their diet was supplemented by small game, pine nuts, wild foods of the desert, including vegetation roots for which they dug with sticks (and thus in the early days these Indians were disparagingly labeled "digger Indians" by white invaders). These shy people in the era of westward expansion were shot on sight for sport; throughout most of the 20th century they have been pushed to struggle against annihilation.

In 1859 the U. S. government agreed to establish for this Paiute band a reservation consisting of the lake, a narrow strip of barren and mountainous country surrounding the lake, and a 17-mile panhandle along the Truckee River which feeds the lake. The Truckee River starts at Lake Tahoe in the High Sierras on the Nevada-California border, and flows almost 100 miles, past Reno, into Pyramid Lake. White squatters by 1865 were encroaching on the lower Truckee River, the reservation's only irrigable land. A century-long struggle in courts and Congress to ban encroachment and secure water rights has ensued.

Though one of the landmark cases in Indian law, *Winters* v. *United States,* handed down in 1908, held that Indians reserved water sufficient for the reservation's purposes from any stream running through or bordering any reservation, the U. S. Department of Interior, trustee for the Pyramid Lake Paiutes, wantonly failed to apply provisions to protect the tribe from unlawful diversion of the Truckee River. In 1905 Derby Dam diverted half the flow of the Truckee to a giant irrigation system to benefit white settlers of the Navada desert. Fish could no longer get up the river to spawn; by 1938 the last of the great Lahontan trout had vanished. By the 1960s Pyramid Lake had shrunk by 60 miles; the pyramid was no longer an island. Anaho Island, home of the last great colony of white pelicans in North America, was accessible to coyotes and other predators who crossed the now-dry land to the rookeries. The most endangered specie, however, was the Pyramid Lake Paiute tribe which depends upon on the lake for subsistence.

Though the Ninth Circuit Court of Appeals in 1981 upheld the right of the tribe to sufficient water, the matter is far from finally resolved. As recently as autumn of 1986 the then-retiring U. S. senator from Nevada, Paul Laxalt, attempted legislation to give congressional approval to the "California-Nevada Water Compact" which would have provided water to state and municipal interests without regard for Indian water rights.

Litigation and lobbying have been devastatingly costly, sorely draining resources of the small tribe. The Episcopal Church's Coalition for Human Needs program has provided certain minor funding assistance, and the Native American Rights Fund, a nonprofit legal service organization, has aided.

Essential to the survival of the Pyramid Lake Paiutes is the Episcopal Church's leadership in attention to shaping public policy to guard the water rights of a small desert tribe which has resided on the shores of a beautiful turquoise lake since time immemorial.

The Utah contrast

The structure of the Episcopal Church is essentially one of a coalition of autonomous dioceses, and the degree to which the Episcopal Church has honored its commitment to bring the gospel to native peoples and the level to which native values and cultural integrity have been honored has depended, basically, on the perspectives of diocesan bishops. A case in point: at almost the same time in the 1920s that Edward Ashley, archdeacon of Niobrara (an appointment made by his bishop), was chairing an ecumenical committee to outlaw Indian dances, in Utah the Episcopal bishop wrote sensitively of the Ute people honoring the church with their turkey dance.

It was 1924 and Arthur W. Moulton, bishop of the Missionary District of Utah, wrote in *Spirit of Missions* about his profound impression at convocation on the Uintah Indian Reservation where Episcopal mission had begun in 1897:

All day they kept driving or riding in — hay racks, buckboards, buggies of ancient vintage, Fords, horses, ponies. They came out of the desert; they came over the mountains; they came from hamlets 50 miles away and from near by. In the middle of the day the medicine man appeared with tents and blankets. A year ago this medicine man would not have a thing to do with us; he refused even to shake hands, but kept his face covered and used his influence against us. But this year he joined us. He joined the crowd; he took part in all the activities; he says we are all right.

At one end of the clearing we built an altar. It was a wonderful altar, with Navajo rugs for the foot pace and the altar steps and the fragrant sage brush massed about the reredos and the wings. On the retable stood the Cross and the candlesticks, and over the Cross hung a large picture of the Redeemer of all mankind. There was never an altar more beautiful, with all its rugged simplicity; no shrine ever more fitted into its surroundings as did this shrine of the sagebrush.

One morning as I was walking across the field I noticed an Indian man standing alone in front of the altar. His hat was in his hand and his head lifted toward the cross. He was a picture indeed — black braided hair, brilliant red shirt, bright blue overalls, yellow moccasins. All alone, he stood there motionless for 20 minutes...I hope and I think that he realized that in the new religion which we were presenting to him was to be found all that was best of his old life and ever so much new inspiration for the days to come.

The new religion, presented according to the rites and doctrines of the Episcopal Church — and perhaps the mode in which it was presented — had a remarkably strong appeal to the Ute people. Tradition has it that the Utes themselves asked the Episcopal Church to come to them, and high in the middle of Mormon country, 90 percent of the people of the Uintah Reservation were at one time Episcopalian. Old records say there had been 800 baptized and 600 presented for confirmation in a 12-year period between 1920 and 1932. The total population of the reservation in 1932 was 1,250. Utes had numbered around 6,000 in 1880. *Indian Tribes and Missions,* published in 1934 by Church Missions Publishing Company, credits the awesome population decrease with "lack of necessities of life in a barren country, plagues of disease, and acts of lawlessness by renegade white men."

In 1925 there were four Episcopal mission centers on the Uintah Reservation: the Church of the Holy Spirit for Indians at Randlett, St. Elizabeth's Mission at Whiterocks, a chapel for Indians at Fort Duchesne which had a hospital and agency office, and at Ouray. Moulton was a "circuit rider" and visited the Uintah Reservation frequently. While bishop-in-charge of Nevada, he was president of Nevada Indian Association which induced Congress to buy land for homes for Indians and persuaded the state legislature to place Indian children in public schools.

In the early 1900s the building was erected for Holy Spirit at Randlett. In the 1920s and 1930s Holy Spirit rendered a unique and badly needed service to the Utes through a farm school. An English couple, Mr. and Mrs. H. O. K. Richards, managed the school and were the first to teach the Utes the art of deep irrigation. Holy Spirit congregation has an unbroken continuity.

St. Elizabeth's at Whiterocks at one time provided religious education for 200 children who attended the nearby government boarding school. Long after the school closed, St. Elizabeth's chapel served the Ute people until it, too, closed in 1978. In the promising renaissance of the late 1980s, St. Elizabeth's reactivated regular worship services.

A new Utah bishop, George Bates, was consecrated in 1986. His earliest statements pledged new emphasis on Indian ministry. Ute people themselves are assuming new leadership in the Episcopal mission. Nancy Pawwinnee has long served as a lay leader at Holy Spirit, and is a former member of the National Committee on Indian Work. The Rev. Quentin Kolb, who left his reservation as a youth, has focused his ministry in urban Salt Lake City. Kolb, a leader in the organization of Mountains and Desert Native American Ministry, was designated as the new coalition's representative to NCIW, and was elected to head the new Urban Indian Episcopal Coalition.

The fledgling Coalition of Mountains and Desert Native American Ministry reflected upon the diminished number of Episcopal missions in the great western inland region in the 20th century; it pondered the vast differences in Indian work priorities from diocese to diocese; it studied differentials in funding support, from clergy salary to base budget support; it contemplated the growing spiritual, social, economic, and health needs of Indian people — all this before asking the Episcopal Church for "freedom from worry that the church will desert us."

Chapter 8

The Episcopal Church's first 100 years in Alaska

In the long winter nights there is a story told about a man named Vine-ee-khaak'aa who long, long ago journeyed by dog team from his home at Arctic Village to Old Rampart House, the Hudson's Bay Company post on the Porcupine River in the vast interior of Alaska. Here he traded furs and caribou hides to an Anglican missionary for Bibles, prayer books and hymn books. Back in his village, surrounded by high mountains of the Brooks Range, an isolated and indigenous church was begun.

The stories say Vine-ee-khaak'aa was the first Christian leader. The seventh was Albert Tritt, a visionary who encountered God and spent three years in retreat and prayer with only the Bible and prayer book. When he emerged from the retreat, he became a leader, first in his community, then moving in the manner of St. Paul, from village to village along the Upper Yukon River to build churches. When he began work on the first church building at Arctic Village, the community gathered around and expressed much curiosity about the steeple. He explained to the puzzled villagers that the steeple on the building was a spear or arrow aimed to heaven to carry their prayers.

Eventually, this Athabascan apostle built churches in the neighboring villages of Chalkytsik and Venetie. In the 1920s a prophecy by a man named Dich'i'zyaa was fulfilled when Albert Tritt was ordained to the diaconate.

Almost from the beginning of the Alaskan mission, the Episcopal Church, recognizing the centrality of the Holy Eucharist in the life of the church, sought means to assure presence of ordained clergy to celebrate this sacrament. Formidable climate and distance meant that presence of conventionally trained and ordained white mission priests among the scattered Native villages would be sporadic. Early in his tenure, the first bishop of Alaska ordained a well-instructed Indian, William Loola, to conduct regular worship services. The Alaskan succession in the episcopacy, recognizing necessity for resident priests to live the faith daily in the midst of the people, initiated fundamental change in clergy ordination requirements in the Episcopal Church. Out of Alaska came the pattern for new ordination procedures known as Canon 8 (now Canon 11), which relate to such remote, small and culturally distinct communities.

Today, approximately half of the 4,600 communicants in the vast Diocese of Alaska — an area twice the size of Texas — is either American Indian or Inuit (Eskimo). Twenty-eight predominantly Alaskan native congregations are scattered along the Yukon River and its tributaries in the Interior Deanery, and along the northern coastal region, from Nome to Barrow, in the Arctic Coast Deanery. Many of the Alaskan Native communicants of the diocese also worship in 20 mixed congregations from Anchorage southward.

Episcopal mission and ministry among the Native peoples of Alaska began in the summer of 1887, a decade before the Alaska Gold Rush, when two Episcopal missionaries arrived at the Athabascan Indian settlement of Anvik, 450 miles upstream from the mouth of the Yukon River, to establish the "Mother Church of Alaska." Mission in Alaska began in the pattern of the old nongeographic jurisdiction of Niobrara as mission among Native peoples. The Alaska mission differed from Niobrara in that the Alaska program brought desperately needed medical care to the Native peoples as well as Christianity and education. Traders and whalers had brought devastation to the native population. For instance, among the Eskimo of the far north, foreign diseases introduced by the whaling industry had swept away whole villages, and alcohol took a continuing high toll.

Native peoples of Alaska are not only culturally and linguistically diverse, as are Native peoples of the "lower 48," but there are also racial distinctions. The Eskimo and the Aleut are not classified as American Indian. The Athabascan Indians were native to the interior along the Yukon River and its many tributaries, and the Tlingit and Haida Indians to the more moderate coastal climate of southeast Alaska.

The first major hurdle confronting the American missionaries was language. For instance, the Athabascan people spoke 58 different dialects. The Lord's Prayer translated at Tanana was not understood 100 miles upriver. The Native peoples had no written language, so the missionaries had first to develop written languages for the many dialects, then teach the Native people how to read them. Episcopal missionaries had their work made easier in some places because of earlier Canadian Anglicans who had done some translations.

Russian Orthodox influence

The Russian Orthodox, almost a century before the arrival of Episcopal missionaries, had first brought the gospel to Alaska. Catherine, empress of all the Russias, in 1788 signed an imperial order sending missionaries to her American colonies. Archimandrite Josaph led a group of 10 monks from the Valaam Monastery in Russia to Alaska in 1794. Five years later he was consecrated bishop of the Russian Orthodox Church for work in Alaska, but drowned in a shipwreck on his way back to Alaska. Among the first wave of Orthodox missionaries was Fr. Herman who dedicated his life to the Aleuts on Spruce Island in Kodiak. The Aleuts called him "Apa," or grandfather. Fr. Herman was later canonized as a saint of the Orthodox Church. One of the original group of monks was Fr. Juvenal who became the first Russian Orthodox martyr when he was killed by hostile Natives. The Orthodox Church also canonized the first Native American saint, Peter, the Aleut. It was in the early 19th century, when the Russian church was establishing missions in California, and 14 Orthodox Aleuts were imprisoned by the Spanish Jesuits, who demanded that the Aleuts accept the Roman Catholic faith. The Aleuts refused, and Peter, the Aleut, is said to have bled to death following torture.

In 1796, on Kodiak, the Orthodox built their first church. The Orthodox priests are said to have baptized 12,000 native people by the end of the 18th century. The Russian church chose Sitka in the southeast as the site for its first church building on the Alaska mainland. The church became St. Michael's Cathedral and Ivan Venianimof became the first bishop to serve in Alaska. In 1858 he was recalled to Russia where he eventually became the Patriarch of Moscow, the highest office of the Russian church.

Notwithstanding the fact that an estimated 48,000 Aleuts perished in the first 50 years of Russian rule, Russian Orthodox influence among Alaskan Natives was momentous. As recently as the 1970s the Orthodox Church was referred to as the "national church" among the Aleuts. Dr. R. Pierce Beaver, in his 1979 survey of Native American and Christian Churches, reported that the Orthodox Church claimed 22,000 Native communicants, almost wholly in Alaska. The Alaskan author, Tay Thomas, estimated in 1967 that there were 96 Orthodox Native congregations. After Russia sold the colony to the United States in 1867, support continued from the Russian Orthodox Church for Alaska Native mission until the 1917 revolution. Many Native people bear Russian surnames.

By the middle 1800s, the Russian Orthodox mission to Alaska had established bilingualism as its norm; Alaska Native languages were used liturgically and in the schools. Dr. Sheldon Jackson, the Presbyterian who eventually became superintendent of education for Alaska, insisted that Alaska Natives could not become Christian until they had been acculturated or "civilized," and the first step toward "civilizing" was eradication of the native languages. Orthodox dictum did not require Natives to become Russians in order to become Christians. Radically divergent Christian philosophy was imposed on Native Alaskans with the arrival of western Christianity, and primal religious traditions — present in the Americas for 30,000 years — have only within recent decades been re-examined by Christian theologians in quest of reconciliation.

The contradiction between Eastern Orthodox and western protestant theory stems from basic theological differences — the Orthodox belief that all things were fulfilled in Christ, not replaced by Christ. Some groups of western protestant Christianity, led by Dr. Jackson, held an irreconcilable interpretation of the gospel. Thus, during the first hundred years of Russian missionizing the traditional cultures were "baptized" into a "newness of life," not discarded and replaced by alien cultures. When western Christianity arrived following the Alaska purchase, the Alaska Native was victim of deep separation between eastern and western theology.

Church of England mission

Anglican influence predated arrival of the Episcopal mission among Alaskan Natives. A highly individualistic Englishman, William Duncan, answered an ad placed by the Church Missionary Society of England for a missionary to the warring Tsimshian Indians along the Canadian Northwest Coast. A former dry goods clerk, Duncan possessed no theological training but had deep religious convictions. He arrived at Fort Simpson in 1857 and set about establishing a "Christian village" at old Metlakatla, Canada, which eventually grew to a population of 1,000 Indians and flourished for 30 years.

His English church benefactors became uneasy about Duncan's informality in worship, and his position on the sacraments of Baptism and Holy Eucharist. Tay Thomas credits Duncan's reluctance to teach his charges about the sacrament of Holy Communion as the Body and Blood of Jesus Christ as stemming from his sensitivity to potential misinterpretation by a people recently converted from cannibalistic ways. While his Christian village concept would serve a century later as a model for economic self-sufficiency, Duncan's informality in relation to the faith caused considerable concern to the Church Missionary Society and the Anglican Church of Canada. Duncan, with the help of Episcopal Bishop Phillips Brooks of Massachusetts and Dr. Henry Ward Beecher, gained audience with President Grover Cleveland and congressional leaders. They granted Duncan and the Metlakatla colony refuge on any Alaskan island they chose. Over 800 Tsimshian Indians, led by Duncan, departed Canada and moved to the "new Metlakatla" on Annette Island in 1887. An informal relationship existed between Duncan's mission and the Episcopal Church — Bishop Rowe baptized the Metlakatla children — but eventually, in 1941, the Metlakatla Christian Mission affiliated with the Methodists.

Church of England missionaries entering from Canada first brought the gospel along the Yukon River to the Athabascan Indians. By 1862 the Canadians had arrived at the old town of Fort Yukon, established as the western outpost of Hudson's Bay Company. Archdeacon Robert McDonald, a Scotsman, spent 50 years in Canada working among Yukon Indians. He and Bishop

William C. Bompas of the Canadian Diocese of Selkirk, made regular visits to Fort Yukon, located eight miles north of the Arctic Circle, and as far down the Yukon as the village of Tanana, 500 miles from Canadian territory.

Serving the archdeacon, from 1881 until his death in 1885, was a young English priest, Vincent C. Sim, whose esteemed influence is yet raised up a full century after his early death in the memory and stories of Episcopal Native clergy along the Yukon. Born in Windsor, England, he was assigned to the mission at Fort Chipewyan in northern Canada, and subsequently appointed assistant to Archdeacon McDonald, who sent the young clergyman to the distant outpost, Old Rampart House, the Hudson's Bay Company trading post on the Upper Porcupine River. Surveys in 1889 determined that the old trading post lay within American territory, but it was from this westernmost mission of the Canadian church that Sim operated. It was here he died.

From Old Rampart House Sim set off on two historic journeys traveling by birch bark canoe and skin boat to bring the gospel to the Athabascan peoples along the Yukon and Tanana Rivers. His 1883 and 1884 journeys covered 2,300 miles, taking him to preach and teach at places where no missionary had ever been. In his letters, he reported how eager the people were for the gospel, sometimes keeping him up all night. In his last letter he wrote:

Along the greater portion of this river the Indians are longing for the Gospel and receive the Word with joy.

His letters also recorded a great epidemic sweeping through the Native fishing camps along the rivers. Possibly diphtheria, the epidemic took a dreadful toll. Sim sometimes found only two or three survivors in a whole village. Of one village, he wrote: "We here found a man with two women and a child, the sole survivors of a small band of Indians who were carried off by the sickness in the summer of 1882." During the winter of 1884-85, from Rampart House, Sim's letters told that hunting was poor and the sickness continued in the land. Sim kept busy teaching, caring for the sick, and building a church at the post. He pleaded for more help:

The Upper Yookon taxes all my energies & with the still greater field of work on the Lower Yookon laying upon me, I feel the burden is greater than I can bear. Do Christian people at home really realize the state of things here?

The *Alaskan Epiphany* in its summer 1985 issue memorializes the young English missionary in an article entitled: "Vincent C. Sim...One of the First."

It was springtime now...and the young priest was dying. Weakened to the point of exhaustion by his travels and caring for the sick around him, he now would share in their way of dying as he had shared in their way of living. Through the window of the rough cabin he lay in, the newly built mission church could been seen. Spring had come to the land, bringing along warm days of blue sky and sunshine, ducks and geese landing on some of the thawed lakes, and the promise of summer — but by now he was oblivious to it all.

...He would die here, among those with whom he had worked and taught. They had taught him too, of course, how to survive and how to live in this land. They had accompanied him on his travels and now, for this last journey, they would care for him too. Perhaps one of those caring for him, there in the little cluster of cabins in the high canyons of the Porcupine River, was a tall young man, noted among his people for his wrestling ability. The tall young man would remember the priest from faraway England.

As the ice on the river broke, and the water began to run once more on the Porcupine...the young priest died. He was laid to rest in the Indian graveyard — a quiet, secluded spot on the top of a high hill. A neat rail and headboard were made and placed by an Indian around the grave. The name carved on the headboard read: "The Reverend Vincent C. Sim." He was barely 30 years old. He was one of the first.

The young Indian man, known among his people for his wrestling skills, would tell his son stories on long Alaskan winter nights about this English priest. The son would listen and learn about the ministry of this Englishman among the Athabascan peoples, and the son in 1962 would become the first Athabascan ordained to the priesthood — David Salmon of Chalkytsik.

At the time of the young priest's death, another Englishman was journeying to the United States, beginning an odyssey that would ultimately lead him to Alaska. His name was Hudson Stuck, and he would become the archdeacon of the Yukon. Many years later Stuck landed the Episcopal launch *Pelican* at the deserted site of Old Rampart House. He climbed the hill and pushed through the grass to the graveyard. He

Let it be remembered to the honour of the Church of England that she had sons and sent them into the wilderness long ago; upon whose labours we of the American Church have tardily entered in these more comfortable times, to reap, in some measure, the fruit.

The Comity Agreement

The Presbyterians had arrived in the southeast in 1877 and under the dynamic Dr. Jackson, who would eventually occupy the highest position of his denomination, major education programs for the native people were begun. Jackson soon realized that his denomination could not singularly educate all

Alaskan Natives. The U. S. government had assumed scant responsibility, so he sought out other denominations to provide teachers in different areas. While historians disagree on whether such a meeting ever happened, it is said that in the early 1880s an interdenominational meeting was held in Philadelphia out of which came an ecclesiastical "nonaggression pact." The Episcopalians agreed to take on work begun by the Anglicans along the upper Yukon and the interior, and to help the Presbyterians along the Arctic Coast. Generally speaking, the rest of the enormous territory was apportioned thusly: the Methodists got Unalaska and the Aleutian Islands; the Baptists got Kodiak; the Congregationalists got Cape Prince of Wales region; the Moravians got the Kuskokwin region; the Roman Catholics received the mid and lower Yukon. The Presbyterians, by the comity agreement, would continue their work in the southeast and extend work to the Arctic coast.

For reasons unknown, the Lutheran Church, which had maintained mission at Sitka in Russian America, was not a party to the agreement. Also conspicuously absent from the agreement were the Orthodox, who had been evangelizing Natives for most of a century and had 11 priests and 16 deacons at work in Alaska at the time of the U. S. purchase in 1867.

Each of the denominations of the comity agreement transported to Alaska the standard model of mission school education that they had rehearsed among the nations and tribes of the contiguous states. The bilingual schools of Russian America had attempted to build on indigenous talent and potential; the Americans built schools with intent to destroy Native languages and cultures. Many Alaska Native families, along with countless American Indian families of the lower states, have their set of sad handed-down stories of punishment for having spoken their own languages and dialects in mission and government boarding schools. Switching, spanking, strapping, paddling, and whipping — corporal punishment rarely practiced by Native American parents — were broadly administered in boarding schools to even the smallest of children as punishment for having spoken native languages though the child likely came from a non-English speaking home. Such was the experience of my gentle and serene mother, Samantha, at Wheelock Academy in the Choctaw country of Oklahoma.

Exceptions deserve note. Hudson Stuck's diaries tell that he had a raging argument at Fort Yukon with territorial school officials over preservation of the native languages. The archdeacon was trying to get permission of the government officials to hold classes in the school in the evenings to teach the native languages which he sensed were dying out. The bureaucrats denied permission. The territorial schools, unmindful of the seasonal cycle of autumn moose hunting and spring muskrat camps, instituted compulsory attendance in the standard terms, thus requiring families to remain stationary in the village from September through May.

Alaska's first Episcopal bishop

In 1888 Alaska was made a missionary district though at the time there was but a single mission established within the gigantic territory. It was not until 1895 that a bishop for the district was consecrated. By then only two Episcopal missions were established, one among the Athabascan on the Yukon and one among the distant Eskimo on the Arctic coast. The man chosen as the first bishop of Alaska, Peter Trimble Rowe, had been born in Canada, and few men had training in their early ministry which so thoroughly fitted them for their life work. His first ministry had been on a Canadian Indian Reserve on the shores of Lake Huron where traveling was done by small boats in summer and by snowshoes in winter. In Alaska, he would travel by boat, snowshoes and dog sled. He spent many wintry days "mushing" with a dog team, usually alone. He once made a 350-mile solo journey from Fairbanks to Valdez, camping out at night in minus 60-degree temperature. The trip took 18 days.

During Rowe's incredibly long tenure — from 1895 until 1942 — he saw standard transportation come from "mushing" by dog team to river transportation aboard the Pelican, and finally to air travel across his giant jurisdiction. He flew with the daring bush pilots in the 1920s, and in 1927 made his first commercial plane flight from Nome to Point Hope in one day; it had once taken him three weeks to make the trip by dog sled.

The unidentified author of the 1925 publication, *Indian Tribes and Missions,* ventured to characterize the distances, size and contrasts of the missionary jurisdiction of Alaska:

> *The vast geographical compass of our Alaskan missions can be seen in the fact that from Point Hope, one of the bleakest and most desolate inhabited places on the face of the earth, to Metlakatla, with the climate of Virginia, the distance in a straight line is about 1,500 miles, half the distance from the Atlantic to the Pacific of the 48 states of the Union. So great is the Jurisdiction of the Bishop of Alaska.*

When selected for the Alaska post, Rowe had understood that his work would be almost entirely among the Native peoples. However, the Alaska gold rush forever changed the face of Alaska and the bishop shortly realized that his ministry would also include the horde of caucasians — the stampeders — who flooded into the area seeking instant riches. So, at the turn of the century, after having established 13 churches, eight schools and three hospitals, the bishop cast about for capable assistance.

Hudson Stuck: archdeacon of the Yukon

The bishop recruited a most capable individual, Hudson Stuck, and named him archdeacon of the Yukon. English by birth, the 40-year-old Stuck was dean of St. Matthew's Cathedral in Dallas, Texas, when he was called to spend the rest of his life in Alaska. A highly versatile man, he wrote five books which are still standards for study of Alaska mission. Ever the defender of Native Alaskans, he eloquently pleaded for restoration of the Indian name, Denali, for Mount McKinley.

Tay Thomas in her history of Alaska mission work, *Cry in the Wilderness,* published by Alaska Council of Churches in 1967, describes the perspectives of the archdeacon:

> *While Bishop Rowe developed a special kinship with the Alaskan newcomers, Hudson Stuck grew to know and love the Indians in a way almost unmatched by any other missionary. He knew well the problems they faced, he insisted in preserving native customs, skills, clothing and food.*
>
> *He condemned as vicious practice the "Americanizing" of natives for profit. He saw the sale of bright cotton clothing bring money for the traders, but pneumonia to the Indians, and he saw starvation wipe out whole families because the men hunted for furs to sell instead of meat to eat and then spent all their money on liquor. The welfare of the natives was always dear to him — he wanted Alaska saved for native Alaskans.*

Anvik, where Episcopal work began in Alaska

It was in June of 1886 that the Rev. Octavius Parker arrived with his family at the Alaskan coastal trading center of St. Michael, the principal supply depot of the district extending up the Yukon River for 2,000 miles. Recently from the Willamette Valley of Oregon, the young missionary was the first the Episcopal Church sent to Alaska. He had been sent with vague instructions to begin mission among the Athabascan Indians at some point on the Yukon River, but he neither spoke any of the Athabascan languages nor did he have guides. Additionally, St. Michael traders, who abominably exploited the Indians and opposed education for the Native peoples, were hostile to the missionary. *Alaskan Epiphany,* summer, 1987, commemorating the century mark of Episcopal mission in Alaska, reprinted an article by Parker which reveals the traders' anxiety:

> *To educate the Indian was to make him too wise, so that he could see the difference between 30 cents and 11 cents' worth of provisions and a $1.25 for a fox skin.*

A large party of Indians from Anvik came in April of 1887 to trade and invited Parker to establish a mission at their village, 450 miles upriver from the mouth of the Yukon. Meanwhile, a young deacon from New York, John Wight Chapman, had arrived in St. Michael and together the young men traveled to Anvik in July to establish the mother church of Alaska.

The missionaries found that the Anvik villagers knew no English and spoke only Athabascan plus a bit of Russian. For most of the year the villagers lived in underground houses and had only recently given up their stone knives and axes for ones of steel acquired from traders. Chapman in 1912 wrote in *Spirit of Missions:*

> *I suppose that when we began work here in 1887 there was hardly any portion of our country which had been so little affected by civilization. Half a dozen traders and missionaries were scattered along the course of a river two thousand miles long.*
>
> *Our first task, as we saw it, was to become sufficiently acquainted with their language, and at the same time to acquaint them with sufficient English so to establish a means of mutual understanding.*
>
> *Rude buildings for a mission house and a schoolhouse were erected. Later a beginning was made upon a church building, and in 1894 the present Christ Church was completed.*

Parker left the mission after only two years, and Chapman continued the work alone. In 1893 he took furlough and when he returned the following year he brought with him three women — a teacher, Deaconess Bertha Sabine; a medical doctor, identified only as Dr. Glanton; and May, his bride. Anvik was home for the Chapman family for the next 61 years, a record in Alaskan mission history. Henry, son of the Chapmans, became a priest and succeeded his father at the Anvik mission. Henry Chapman returned to Anvik from his retirement home in North Carolina for the centennial celebration at Anvik in July, 1987.

First United Thank Offering

The Women's Auxiliary in 1889 designated $1,000, one-half of the first United Thank Offering, to build Christ Church at Anvik. May Seely Chapman described both her first view of the mission which would be her home for the rest of her life and the first Sunday worship in the new church building in August of 1894:

> *This eventful day had been misty in a fine rain. Anvik landmarks came into sight, idyllic, with white tents and little brown huts set in the green grass, smoke rising from the fires, the scarlet salmon hanging to dry upon the racks, against the silvery green of the willows and the dark spruces. To our left, rose the high rocky bluffs of the Yukon, crowned with thickets of spruce and the feathery birch and alder. Slowly our little steamer rounded the last rocky point. Young natives had come out in their canoes and paddled swiftly all about the boat in welcome.*

The mission premises came into sight, the new little log church with its white belfry and surmounting, the cross. Within, hung the bell, the gift of a devoted churchwoman in New York, probably the first church bell to send its sound across those rivers. There were the storehouses, and the sawmill, more useful than a gold mine to the mission, and the gambrel roofed log building where school was held. Our own log cabin home, set high upon the hill.

Just then, as the boat came to the land, the clouds parted, the sun shone out, and a rainbow, a rare sight in that latitude, stood above our new home welcoming us at the end of our 6,000 mile journey. We went up the paths, through the groups of waiting people, into the cabin, and knelt to give thanks and to ask a blessing upon the new life upon which we were entering.

We went into the church. The logs had been cut, and the foundation tiers laid, before Mr. Chapman had left in the summer previous. The native men had given one day at cutting logs without pay, and when the foundation was completed, the Doxology had been sung. The walls were raised by the native men voluntarily. . .the building was completed by Maurice Johnson, a Swede, and he had done careful and substantial work. The room was 25 feet square, and there was no furniture excepting the handsome stone font, given by our faithful friends of the Women's Auxiliary in Newark, and the small Estey organ from Vermont.

Sister Bertha found an empty packing box, covered it with turkey red calico and draped it in white, and it was set between the two eastern windows to serve as altar. Its only furniture was a small wooden cross. We found glasses and filled them with the brilliant red spires of the deerweed and the feathery tipped grasses gathered from God's own garden along the river bank in front of the mission, and set them on each side of the cross upon the altar. A large sheet was hung across one corner of the room to serve as a "vestry." Benches had been brought in from the school room and the church was as nearly ready for the service the next day as we could make it.

The people came to the church, 85 persons crowding into the room. The men sat on benches, the women crouched on the floor, abject figures with their hair falling over their downcast faces. The babies were snug in the parki hoods on the backs of the mothers. The toddlers ran about in bright calico shirts, vests like those of their fathers, and blue denim trousers buttoned on with large white agate buttons, a much admired decoration.

Familiar hymns were sung. The men looked up, listening to the

119

*service and the words of the interpreter. When the service was end-
ed, the people still sitting quietly in their places, the minister came
from the vestry and said: "Come, my children." One by one those
boys and girls of that first school came and stood in a semi-circle
before him, to be catechized.*

Although Chapman never ceased to spread the gospel and build up the
church, he also became a dedicated teacher and served as postmaster, radio
operator, dentist, doctor and doer of everything that needed to be done. He
was also a scholar, recording much of the local culture and language, and
contributing papers to anthropological journals for many years.

The UTO funds were well invested. Christ Church at Anvik on the Yukon
continues, after 100 years, to bring the gospel.

Subsequent Yukon River mission

Episcopal mission moved up the Yukon River. The next Athabascan work
was begun in 1891 at Tanana, 800 miles upstream from the coast; then, 200
miles further upstream, the Episcopal missionaries began work at Fort Yukon. The nearer the Episcopal missionaries moved toward the Canadian border
the more groundwork they found prepared for them. At Tanana the Anglicans had made considerable progress in translating The Book of Common
Prayer into the local Athabascan dialect. When the Rev. Jules Prevost arrived
at Tanana, he was able to move rapidly toward extending work. Plying up
and down the river in his little missionary launch, Prevost, during his 15-year
stay as both priest and physician, traveled to 32 native villages and set up
a school. Eventually, he acquired a small printing press, gift of Episcopalians
in the states, and began publishing the first newspaper in the Alaskan interi-
or, the *Yukon Press*. The village of Tanana did not depend on an adjacent
mining camp but owed its existence to a military post, Fort Gibbon. Hudson
Stuck, a frequent visitor to the area, wrote of the animosity between the town
and the military post and noted:

*... regardless of the animosity between them, the town was neces-
sary to the post for two reasons: whiskey and wood. Most of the buildings in Tanana were saloons and civilian employees of the military
post chopped approximately 3,000 cords of wood a year.*

*The evil influence which the town and the army post have exerted
upon the Indians finds its ultimate expression in the growth of the
graveyard and the dwindling of the village.*

The next Episcopal mission in the interior was established at Fort Yukon,
the spot believed by Stuck to be the most important location along the water-
way. Here, furs were brought from a thousand miles away and when Bishop
Rowe first visited Fort Yukon he found 300 Indians living there. It was to

St. Stephen's Mission at Fort Yukon that Rowe sent his dynamic archdeacon, Stuck, who traveled by dog team some 2,000 miles annually supervising 30 churches and missions in the height of the gold rush.

Hudson's Bay Company, clearly violating Russian territory, had established Fort Yukon in 1847. Anglican missionaries arrived in 1862, and the memory of that first service in Fort Yukon still exists in some of the older stories of the area. The Rev. David Salmon, remembering, comments, "I've heard that when Kirkby (the first Anglican missionary) held that first service, he stood on a piece of caribou hide, and all the people gathered. When he pulled out the prayer book, people were fascinated. They'd never seen a book, you know? They didn't know what this was that he had, that was so white. . .and they were fascinated by the noise that the pages made when he turned them."

So, when missionaries of the American church arrived in 1896 at Fort Yukon they found Christianity well-entrenched; the Indians were familiar with the Bible and prayer book in their own languages. St. Stephen's Mission for many years operated Hudson Stuck Memorial Hospital to which Alaska Natives were brought from incredible distances by dog team for treatment.

It was also at St. Stephen's that Bishop Rowe began a pattern in developing indigenous leadership which has long served the scattered native villages. It was here that he ordained the Athabascan, William Loola, to the diaconate. The third bishop of Alaska, William Gordon Jr., would substantially build upon Rowe's design to serve the Alaskan Native population through ordination of indigenous clergy. In earlier days of Episcopal mission in Alaska, the church assigned one priest to serve huge areas and sheer logistics permitted only occasional visits by the priest. Gordon, whose tenure was 1948-1974, in the early 1960s challenged the national church to provide for the ordination of indigenous leaders in the village congregations. By 1964 Gordon was able through revision of the canons to ordain five Native priests — Milton Swan of the Arctic Coast, and Titus Peter, David Salmon, Isaac Tritt and Paul Tritt of the Yukon Valley area.

Other Episcopal missions were founded around the turn of the century along the great river and its tributaries — St. Andrew's at Stephen's Village, where Deaconess Bedell long served; St. John's-in-the-Wilderness at Allakaket, the only mission to serve the two distinct races, Indians and Eskimos; St. Paul's at Eagle, a stone's throw from the Canadian border; Bishop Rowe Chapel at Arctic Village, where Vine-ee-khaak'aa and later Albert Tritt founded the indigenous church; St. Mark's Mission at Nenana, which would become a center for schooling; St. Timothy's at Tanana Crossing, where within a few years after its founding there was scarcely a person who had not turned to the church. A dozen other chapels and congregations have developed in the interior, including work at Fairbanks, the diocesan headquarters. While the gold rush came and went, the Episcopal missions founded around the turn of the century have remained. The archdeacon, in referring to the transients of the gold rush era, is quoted as describing Fairbanks in 1904 as a "town of 10,000 people but no one here to stay."

Instrumental to the work in many of the villages were the Native people who served as lay readers or catechists. Two who were active in Tanana, on the Yukon River, and in Nenana, on the Tanana River, were "Blind David" and "Blind Paul." Though blind, David canoed or poled from village to village to hold services. Arriving in a village, carrying his great stick and a sheep's horn, he would blow the horn when it came time for the service and grandmothers today still remember how everybody would come running at the sound of the horn and how the children would fight for the privilege of holding his stick.

Another early lay reader, William Pitgu (or Pitka) of Rampart, on the Yukon River, moved to Tanana when the church closed in Rampart as the gold rush died and the population declined. His granddaughter, Sally Hudson of Fairbanks, recently commented, "I have always wondered why our Native people accepted the Gospel so readily. . .Why they welcomed it with such devotion and faith. I asked my grandfather that once, when I was a little girl, and he said, in our language, 'We have always known there was a Creator, someone above us, but now, through the Gospel, we know WHO that is. . .our Father, who loves us.'"

First-hand view of Yukon mission

Moses Cruikshank at age eight was put on a boat at Fort Yukon and sent to St. Mark's Episcopal Mission, steaming first down the great Yukon River to Tanana, then up the Tanana River to distant Nenana. In his autobiography, *The Life I've Been Living,* published in 1986 by the University of Alaska, the Athabascan elder springs open a door to allow a glimpse of life in the Episcopal mission schools and Alaska life as it was in the early part of the 20th century. His stories bring a human dimension to larger-than-life figures such as Hudson Stuck, who once fished Moses out of the Yukon River with a pike pole. Young Moses had fallen overboard from the Pelican, the Episcopal craft which plied the Yukon and its tributaries 5,200 miles each summer for many years carrying the missionaries to sprouting towns, widely-flung villages, and countless native summer fishing camps. Among its passengers from time to time were Bishop Rowe and Stuck.

When Moses arrived at St. Mark's Mission in 1913, the archdeacon had just made the world's first climb of Mount Denali (McKinley), the tallest mountain on the North American continent. At the school, Moses was made "dog boy," cooking for and feeding the sled dogs, as well as gathering fresh straw for the dogs' bedding. Later, through hard study and good marks, he vied for a summer job as cleaning boy aboard the Pelican and journeyed with the archdeacon all the way from Fairbanks to the mouth of the Yukon at St. Michael. Later, Moses "mushed" the winter trails with the missionaries. In his autobiography he provides a glimpse of the esteemed deaconess, Harriet M. Bedell, at St. Andrew's Mission, St. Stephen's Village. She eventually departed Alaska to work briefly among the Cheyenne in Oklahoma and for many years among the Seminole in Florida.

In the century since Episcopal mission came among the Indians and Eskimo in Alaska, considerable has been written about the stalwart missionaries who braved the bleak, lonely and frozen north to bring the gospel. But scant has been written from the perspective of the enablers — the Alaskan Natives who interpreted the missionary's sermon, guided his dog-team, tended the dogs, set up camps, cut the wood and ran the boats. Moses Cruikshank's stories describe the archdeacon's invaluable lead dog, Muk, and the near-panic brought on when Muk's tail froze to the ground one night in Nenana. He tells of Gunga Din, another choice sled-dog who got into a fight in Minto with government (GI) dogs and killed two. He tells of going to work as a water boy, at age 12, with the crew building the Alaska Railroad, a venture to provide overland access to the Alaskan interior. The elder retells the stories of his grandfather about the Hudson's Bay Company traders and the gold rush stampeders and the traditional Athabascan ways.

Most significant to an understanding of the Episcopal Church's early mission among Alaskan Natives, Cruikshank, a retired Bureau of Indian Affairs employee, recounts experiences of going to school at the Episcopal missions in Alaska and receiving further education at Mt. Hermon in Massachusetts. He tells of panning for gold, trapping, and driving the nails that built the Episcopal schools and village churches along the Yukon and Tanana Rivers. The BIA broke a precedent in the 1970s and named a school in Beaver for him, the first time a bureau school had been named for a living individual.

Point Hope on the Arctic: site of second mission

Point Hope, to the far north on the Bering Sea, was the site of the second Episcopal mission in Alaska. It was begun by a layman, Dr. John B. Driggs, a physician from Wilmington, Delaware.

Whalers had long plied the Bering Sea and their impact at the coastal town of Point Hope had been devastating to the Eskimo inhabitants. A common practice of traders had been to trade the native people liquor for whale bone, a highly marketable commodity a century ago; fashionable wasp-waisted women required baleen — long flexible strips from the mouth of the bowhead whale — for corset stays. In addition to the moral and spiritual devastation resulting from alcohol introduced by the whalers' trade, the Eskimos were physically devastated by the white men's diseases. Measles swept away whole villages. U. S. Navy officials informed Episcopal authorities of the condition of the natives at Point Hope and urged that a medical missionary be sent. Driggs offered his services and reached Point Hope in July, 1890.

As the doctor stepped ashore, he helplessly watched as the Arctic waves swept away most of his belongings, including his supply of coal. Once settled in a two-room house which would serve as school, dispensary and living quarters, the doctor's next challenge was to persuade the children to come to classes. There is a story that he lured his first pupil with a piece of molasses cake. Popular history has it that Driggs' first pupil was named Kinneeveeuk. Before the year was out, however, 50 children were in his school.

In addition to teaching, Driggs toiled endlessly to care for the ill and he often traveled many miles to outlying hunting camps to tend those too ill to be brought to him. One of this frequent stops, just south of Point Hope, was the village of Kivalina, home decades later of the first Eskimo priest, Milton Swan, who was ordained in 1964.

Driggs ministered at Point Hope for 18 long and lonely years. He weathered countless hardships. Winter came early one year and the supply ship failed to arrive. Fuel and food became a very serious problem. At one time the only food left in the village was a dead walrus which washed ashore during a storm.

A further hardship for the doctor was the lack of companionship with anyone from outside Alaska. It was not until he had spent four unbroken years at the mission that the Episcopal Church sent him an assistant, the Rev. E. H. Edson. By 1908, though the doctor was only 54, his health failed and he was obliged to turn over his mission work to others. The legacy he left lives on. The liquor problem diminished; polygamy disappeared; the status of women and health conditions improved. The school founded by Driggs had equipped Eskimos to protect themselves against unscrupulous whalers and traders. Driggs' goal had been to help people of Point Hope become educated Christian Eskimos, not imitations of the incoming caucasian Christians.

Episcopal mission on the northern Alaska coast, begun by a lonely lay physician, today fans downward from Barrow, Point Lay, Point Hope, Kivalina, Noatak, Kotzebue and Nome.

The reindeer arrival

Aboard the same ship that left Driggs at Point Hope was Dr. Sheldon Jackson, the man responsible for introducing reindeer to the Eskimos. The fiery, five-foot-tall and controversial Presbyterian went on to Barrow where he observed that the Eskimo were facing starvation. Commercial ivory hunters had slaughtered the walrus, whalers were driving the whales beyond the reach of the native skin boat, and seals were being killed for their skins at a rate that would wipe them out in a few years' time. During that same Arctic voyage, Jackson visited the Siberian coast and had observed the reindeer economy of the villagers. He headed for Washington, seeking appropriations to import reindeer to Alaska to save the Eskimos. Though he did not then get a congressional appropriation, he was able to raise enough money through public subscriptions to begin a herd the following summer.

The reindeer experiment was less than instantly successful; the Eskimo had to be trained as herders. At first, natives of Siberia were brought in to teach the Alaskan Natives reindeer husbandry, and when this arrangement did not work out, Jackson went all the way to Norway to bring back 16 Lapp herders to train the Eskimo. The Lapps stipulated that a Lutheran clergyman be provided to attend their spiritual needs and teach their children. The Norwegian Lutheran Synod, at request of the U. S. government, sent Tollef Brevig, a man who lived 18 years among the Eskimo and who became much loved and trusted by them.

While the reindeer project failed to fulfill expectations, the story became a part of the lore of Alaska.

Episcopal Alaskan mission today

The mission at Point Hope in 1948 provided the Diocese of Alaska with its third bishop, the 30-year-old William Gordon, then the youngest to have been elected to the episcopate of the American church. Gordon became an airplane pilot — the churchwomen's blue thank offering boxes paid for a plane — and he soon became familiar with every bush landing strip of the far north. The changes he championed in ordination canons have allowed the Alaskan Church to ordain more than 20 Native clergy in the last 15 years. In 1983 an Alaska Native woman, Anna Frank, was ordained priest; four years later she remained the only Native American woman priest. A mental health counselor, she was ordained deacon by Gordon in 1974. Along with lay-leader Bessie Titus of Minto, she served on commissions and committees of the national church. Frank, who resides in Fairbanks, has brought a significant presence to the Standing Commission on the Church in Small Communities and Titus has provided steadfast direction as an officer of National Committee on Indian Work, and as chairperson for NCIW's Leadership Development Committee. Both were elected as deputies to the 1988 General Convention.

Further development of native leadership — ordained and lay — continues to be a major concern in the gigantic Diocese of Alaska. The two bishops — David R. Cochran and George C. Harris — who have followed Gordon are especially receptive to alternative training for clergy; both were elevated to the episcopate from the post of director of the Dakota Leadership Program of South Dakota, which developed models in leadership training by extension.

The English priest, Roland Allen, advanced fundamentally different strategies for mission and ministry among indigenous people than had been the old colonial model. Allen served as an Anglican missionary to China, 1892-1902, under sponsorship of the Society for the Propagation of the Gospel. His convictions on indigenous mission were considered quite radical. He eventually resigned from parish ministry and spent the last part of his life in Kenya where he wrote extensively and argued to the end that the responsibility for leadership in mission churches be given to indigenous people. Allen proposed that lay people should exercise serious responsibilities, that the church, wherever it is, should be "self-governing, self-supporting and self-propagating," that responsibilities for leadership in mission churches be given to the native people, that the Eucharist is central to the life of the church, and, therefore, clergy must be present to celebrate the Eucharist. The latter opened thought to new approaches for ordination training.

The "Roland Allen model" has served as a pattern — especially for leadership development — in the Episcopal Church's Alaska mission. In 1987, however, that enormous jurisdiction, still had 10 villages without resident native clergy. Some of the Native Alaskan Episcopal community expresses serious concern about need for ordained leaders to serve in a far broader capacity than that of sacramentalist.

Bishop Harris has expressed optimism, stressing that vocations are emerging slowly but surely. The tall and stately, Brooklyn-born, eastern-educated bishop spent the formative years of his ministry as a missionary in the Philippines. In a printed report of the 1983 Pacific Rim conference which examined the legacy of Roland Allen, Harris called for fundamental changes and restructuring of the church at every level of its life, particularly in the area of ordained ministry. He said:

> The majority of parishes and congregations are still serviced by a single, over-worked, priest who, in the absence of a remote and inaccessible bishop, a dearth of fellow-priests, a non-existent diaconate and a passive laity, attempts to carry alone the entire ministerial function of the congregation. Yet, received traditions and inherited structures militate against reform.

Impeded by the sheer vastness of the jurisdiction, the Diocese of Alaska has sought to administer its mission through carving the country into four huge deaneries, each representing a land mass exceeding some provinces of the eastern United States. Study is under way for subdividing the Interior Deanery, where Athabascan priests serve as dean and subdean — Titus Peter and Luke Titus, respectively.

The Alaska Native Advocacy Committee was restructured in 1985 with elected representatives from each of the four deaneries. Three of the deanery-designated representatives — Elsie Pitka, Interior Deanery; Donald Peter, South Central Deanery; Monte Littlefield, Southeast Deanery — participated along with Ms. Titus in the land-mark Oklahoma II Consultation of 1986.

Though many of the interior villages are almost 100 per cent Episcopalian, the church was unable to take a position on the imminent congressional legislation determining status of Alaskan Natives in relation to their lands after 1991. The Alaska Native Claims Settlement Act of 1971 required new legislation after 20 years. Varying positions on how to deal with the issue have polarized Native communities and organizations, and so the church at large could take no position. Donald Peter, an Alaska Native lay leader who lives in Anchorage and serves as an officer of the Alaska Native Advocacy Committee, recently spoke his viewpoint on the role of the church in the 1991 issue: "Perhaps the Church's role is to be what it has always been in our villages — a center and a place of healing. Instead of taking a position, maybe the Church's role is to be the one place where we can come together, despite our differences, and be one, and find healing from the scars that are inevitably going to result from however all this turns out."

Spiritual renewal is a significant characteristic of today's ministry among Native Alaskans; joyful singing fills the air at Episcopal gatherings in the brief summer season of the midnight sun. And during the long winter nights, stories are yet told of Vine-ee-khak'aa and the others who long, long ago traded caribou hides for copies of the Holy Bible and Anglican prayer book and set about independently in the shadows of the high mountains of the Brooks Range at Arctic Village to build an indigenous church.

William Loola of Fort Yukon was the first Alaska Native to be ordained deacon, in 1903.

Chapter 9

The national church in Indian ministry from the 1960s forward

One hundred years after General Convention first deemed evangelization among American Indians as a mission imperative and voted to establish the Missionary District of the Niobrara, the internationally recognized Standing Rock Sioux author, Vine Deloria Jr., wrote a document called *More Real Involvement.* This 1968 work laid groundwork for today's structure of Native American ministry within the national church. The document strongly called for more involvement of Indian people in Indian ministry decision-making. Deloria, son and grandson of Episcopal priests, wrote, "We seek the right to devise and direct programs which will fit our basic needs and communities in the life and program of the Episcopal Church."

In 1958 General Convention had ordered a special study of the church's Indian work policy; in 1961 the Detroit General Convention passed nine resolutions on Indian work. There was still, however, no mandate for self-determination, a transition from being recipients to participants in the life of the church.

The National Advisory Committee on Indian Work: 1965-1967

Outgrowth of the Detroit convention resolution were a blue-ribbon National Advisory Committee on Indian Work and a well written report entitled *The American Indian in the Mission and Ministry of the Episcopal Church.* A variety of distinguished Native Americans were named to this advisory panel and a listing is included as appendix VI.

The report of the committee pointed out that structural separation had contributed to the isolation of Indian work and workers, even within their own jurisdictions.

> . . . *it is clear that this (Indian) work has been structurally separated from the general pattern of the Church's life and growth. This separation appears to be the result of precedent set in the days of the missionary frontier when bishops and clergy "went West" and were supported by parishioners and dioceses "back home."*
>
> *This pattern was institutionalized in the form of basic appropriations made by General Convention and sent to the missionary districts or dioceses. New programs and services developed by Executive Council and within jurisdictions over the past 25 years have touched the Indian field only in oblique ways. . .developments within the Indian world have had little bearing on the life of the wider Church. . .*

The church was called to strengthen its ministry and services and its commitment to mission and outreach among American Indians in reservation communities, in rural areas, and in towns and cities. The church was called to respond to the deepening social and spiritual needs of Indian people, to development of leadership committed to work for creative response to those needs. Recommendations spoke to public policy, social action, regional coordination, and new patterns for the funding of work proposed.

More real involvement (late 1960s)

Shortly after Deloria was elected in 1968 to Executive Council, he contacted numerous American Indian clergy and laity throughout the country, eliciting from them their perspectives on how the resolutions of the 1961 General Convention could best be implemented. The consensus statement from Indian leaders, presented to the Most Rev. John E. Hines, and the Executive Council, called for

1. A special conference of American Indian and Eskimo clergy of the United States and Canada, to explore mutual concerns and to design an ongoing program for church work in the field of Indian affairs in which the maximum responsibility and policy-making would be placed in Indian hands.

2. That an Indian desk be established to coordinate all programs of Indian concerns, locally, regionally and nationally. A proviso was included that the Rev. Clifford Samuelson, who had heretofore headed the Indian program at Church Center, train an Indian person to assume the position of executive secretary.

3. That a National Advisory Committee of American Indian Churchmen be appointed immediately upon creation of the Indian Desk.

4. That a pastor-at-large be appointed to minister to American Indian people in all parts of the country — reservations, urban centers, and surviving communities east of the Mississippi, etc.; and that Indian people choose this pastor-at-large.

5. That the national church continue substantial aid and support to Indian work through regular appropriations to the dioceses and missionary districts unable to finance such work without national assistance BUT that each diocese and missionary district BE REQUIRED to give evidence of:

   a) Joint planning with Indian people through church and community organizations.

b) Indian participation in the direction and administration of church programs.

c) Provisions for the development of Indian leadership in the diocese, both clergy and lay.

6. That American Indian people be included on all church commissions and committees.

Five other points of the *More Real Involvement* statement spoke to leadership development, including seminary curricula, recruitment, training, and alternative approaches to training.

The Executive Council at its December, 1968, meeting authorized a 1969 conference, establishment of a National Advisory Committee of American Indian Churchmen, and a program to meet the urgent need for an indigenous ministry, ordained and lay, among American Indians and Alaska Natives.

Two months later, the February, 1969, Executive Council passed a resolution affirming the self-determining voice of American Indians, the need for indigenous leadership, alternative modes of training, and consideration of Indian persons for appointment to posts and committee assignments. The February meeting, however, deemed that the National Committee on Indian Work would not necessarily be composed of American Indians, and specified appointment of five bishops. The resolution pointed out that the Episcopal Church was then spending $1.7 million annually (approximately $900,000 from national church budget) "but often not as effectively as possible and therefore a process of examination and development of new directions, styles and priorities needs to be set in motion." The resolution also stipulated that while the Presiding Bishop would consult with the NCIW about the Indian person to be on staff, his would be the final decision. No mention was made of the pastor-at-large.

A new national church funding configuration emerged in 1970 with formation of a coalition of 14 aided western dioceses. Coalition 14 would effect Native American mission to a major degree.

Printed documents and booklets issued in 1970 and stored in the Austin, Texas, archives include *American Indians and Eskimos: Their Major Needs, Problems and Opportunities,* and an attractive booklet, *This Land Is Our Land: The American Indian in American Society 1970.* They call for Indian/Eskimo self-determination, support for ongoing work of the church, an Indian/Eskimo scholarship fund, Native leadership development and training, reconciliation of reservation/rural and urban communities, strengthening of tribal government, cultural studies, and ecumenicity.

National Committee on Indian Work
Records do not exist of an organizational meeting of the National Committee

on Indian Work. An undated printed report — thought to be from the early 1970s — entitled *Ministry to American Indians* lists a Sioux and former Bureau of Indian Affairs official, Kent FitzGerald, as executive secretary of the National Committee on Indian Work. Mrs. Elizabeth Clark Rosenthal is listed as research editor.

Members of what is thought to be the first NCIW were:

Officers: The Rev. George A. Smith, chairman, and the Rev. Webster Two Hawk, vice chairman.

Indian members: Alaska — The Rev. Titus Peter (Athabascan) and Alfred Grant (Athabascan); Great Lakes — The Rev. George A. Smith (Chippewa) and Mrs. Joycelyn Ninham (Oneida-Stockbridge). Great Plains: The Rev. Webster Two Hawk (Sioux) and the Rev. Innocent Goodhouse (Sioux); Southwest — Oscar Lee House (Navajo-Oneida) and Francis Riggs (Cheyenne).

Bishop members: William J. Gordon Jr., Missionary District of Alaska (Bishop Gordon succeeded Conrad H. Gesner of South Dakota on Gesner's retirement in 1970); C.J. Kinsolving II, Diocese of New Mexico and Southwest Texas; George T. Masuda, Missionary District of North Dakota; Philip F. McNairy, Diocese of Minnesota, and Chilton Powell, Diocese of Oklahoma.

Dr. Howard Meredith (Cherokee) of Oklahoma replaced FitzGerald in 1973 as executive secretary for NCIW. A Province VIII field consultant, Joan Boardman, was hired. In 1976 a proposal for a separate Diocese of Navajoland was offered at General Convention; convention modified it and created Navajoland Area Mission. Meredith was succeeded by Fayetta Knight (Seneca-Cayuga), also of Oklahoma.

In 1977 Clyde Red Shirt (Oglala Sioux) from the Pine Ridge Reservation in South Dakota was named NCIW executive director. A reorganization of NCIW occurred in late November, 1977, when a team of 15 American Indians headed by Dr. Helen Peterson (Oglala Sioux) met in Denver.

The following spring a new National Committee on Indian Work was appointed and included:

George Abrams (Seneca), Owanah Anderson (Choctaw), Belle Beaven, Fr. Wilbur Bears Heart (Sioux), Fr. Ron Campbell (Sioux), Fr. Innocent Goodhouse (Sioux), Thomas Jackson (Navajo), the Rt. Rev. Walter Jones, Norman Nauska (Athabascan), Kenneth Owen (Sioux), the Rt. Rev. Frederick Putnam, Helen Peterson (Sioux), Ross Swimmer (Cherokee), and Fr. Webster Two Hawk (Sioux).

The new NCIW reviewed the *More Real Involvement* document and determined that most points raised a decade previously were still valid and not yet fully met. In establishing new goals and objectives, NCIW established as the number one priority training for ordained leadership among Indian people. Strengthening of ministry among Native Americans and communication were lifted up as essential; legislative advocacy was identified as a critical need. The NCIW elected Owanah Anderson chairperson.

Succeeding Red Shirt as executive secretary in 1979 was Steve Charleston (Choctaw), who had graduated from the Episcopal Divinity School but had not yet been ordained. Specific growth occurred in the early 1980s in the area of leadership development. Charleston resigned the NCIW post in 1982 and was subsequently ordained to the priesthood. He was succeeded by Alan Sanborn (Penobscot) at Church Center and Owanah Anderson, after serving as field consultant for a year, became staff officer for Native American ministries in 1984. After several years' effort, spearheaded by Province VI, a field staff position for Native ministries was approved in 1983. Two Sioux men briefly served in the position: Fr. Virgil Foote (Dakota) of Minnesota and Sherman Wright (Rosebud Sioux) of South Dakota. In the autumn of 1986, Dr. Carol Hampton (Caddo) was appointed to the post and established the Indian Ministries Field Office in Oklahoma City.

Coalition 14

The process through which major national church funding for Indian mission flowed, beginning in 1970, was shortly identified by the acronym, C-14, for Coalition 14. This coalition of western dioceses which required annual base budget support from the National Church was allocated a substantial block grant, and through a process of challenge and accountability, the dioceses apportioned the grant among themselves.

The coalition by 1987 had digressed considerably from its original focus and had begun a process for a re-visioning. Many of the original member dioceses have become self-supporting, though several have chosen to remain within the coalition from a sense of partnership and for mutual support. New dioceses have joined the coalition. Others have left. Of the 16 member dioceses of 1987, seven are non-aided. Four have major Indian work. Five have Indian work limited to a single reservation or congregation, and of those five, two (Nevada and Wyoming) receive no funding through C-14.

In 1987 Coalition 14 received from the national church through the National Mission of Church in Society an allocation of $1,415,527. Four dioceses with major Native American work — Alaska, Navajoland, North and South Dakota — received 79 per cent of the allocation.

Coalition 14 members are Alaska, *Arizona, Eastern Oregon, *Eau Claire, Idaho, Montana, Navajoland, *Nevada, North Dakota, *Northern Michigan,

*Rio Grande, *San Joaquin, South Dakota, Utah, Western Kansas, and *Wyoming.

* denotes non-aided dioceses

C-14/NCIW joint consultations on Indian ministry

Two major consultations on Native American ministry, jointly sponsored by C-14 and NCIW, were held in Oklahoma City in 1984 and 1986. Echoing the *More Real Involvement* statement of the 1960s, both consultations called for greater empowerment of Indian peoples in decision-making levels of the Episcopal Church.

Among the recommendations from the first consultation was for NCIW members to be designated for appointment by constituency, and for all dioceses which have a significant Native American population to establish diocesan Indian committees. By 1987 all NCIW members were representatives of, and accountable to, a diocesan Indian committee or urban congregation and four new diocesan Indian committees have either emerged or been reactivated. Additionally, the Province VIII Indian Commission has broadened its outreach and program with a primary focus on development of new urban Indian ministry in western cities.

Responding to the anti-Indian backlash which poses a new threat to Indian treaty rights, new emphasis has been placed on legislative advocacy and new energy has been directed toward combatting racism.

The Covenant of Oklahoma II

The second NCIW/C-14 joint consultation developed guidelines for new approaches to Native American ministry when 84 Episcopal leaders from 13 dioceses spent a week vigorously scrutinizing present mission and ministry. Thirteen bishops were present, including the Presiding Bishop. Almost two-thirds of the participants were Native American. A document developed at the consultation, called Covenant of Oklahoma II, cited seven action items which need to be addressed, including empowerment, racism, media, curriculum development and native spirituality.

While acknowledging that racism "is still a hideous reality in our midst," the covenant nevertheless is framed positively and hopefully and calls for examination of alternative modes of church governance and structure and attention to native ordained and lay leadership development. (See appendix IV.)

Native American leadership development

In the early 1970s a survey among seven major Christian denominations with 499 Indian congregations revealed that the seven had only 68 ordained American Indians in the field. To respond to the clergy shortage, the Native American Theological Association was organized in 1978. Headed by Dr.

Howard Anderson, the five-denomination NATA developed special education programs and seminary affiliates.

Hearing an imperative from the grass roots constituency on the need for trained Christian leaders, NCIW sought alternatives in models for education and looked to ecumenical models for assistance. While NCIW's budget was modest, a large percentage of it was allocated to the Minneapolis-based Native American Theological Association and Cook Christian Training School in Tempe, Arizona.

In the mid-1980's, after having almost exclusively relied on NATA and Cook Christian Training School, NCIW noted in the spring of 1986 that not one Episcopal Indian was in seminary. On the invitation of Seabury-Western Theological Seminary, a group of Native and non-Native leaders met and developed the Evanston Covenant, envisioning a center of Native American theological study at the Illinois seminary. NCIW pledged substantial funding to the program and seven Indian postulants were on the campus in autumn of 1986.

New leadership — new vision

The new Presiding Bishop has given extraordinary attention to Native American ministry. During his first 18 months he visited Navajoland, attended the Oklahoma Consultation, participated in the Niobrara and Minnesota-North Dakota-Eau Claire convocations, met with the National Committee on Indian Work, and visited the Denver Urban Native American Congregation. In response to the call for inclusion of Native Americans in decision-making, and out of his own sense of inclusivity, Browning appointed 18 Native Americans — a record number — to national committees, boards and commissions. Within weeks after his installation he appointed a Blue Ribbon Task Force on Indian Affairs, charged with advising him on how to respond to the spiritual needs as well as the social and legal justice concerns of the Native American.

As the Browning era mission imperatives are fine-tuned and offered to General Convention in July 1988, Native American Episcopalians in larger numbers than ever previously will be deputies to convention.

The NCIW has recently developed its own set of Mission Imperatives:

> To share the ministry of Christ reflecting the unique cultural heritage of American Indians and Alaska Natives.

> To represent the spirit of the Episcopal Church through servanthood and its proclamation of the gospel of Jesus Christ.

> To develop and nurture leadership skills leading to the empowerment of American Indians/Alaska Natives.

> To foster improved communications between American Indian/Alaska Natives and other people.

To foster improved communications between American Indian/Alaska Natives and other people.

Casting off shackles of dependency, Episcopal Native Americans are, after 400 years, at the brink of assuming a partnership role. We have developed new networks and coalitions, shared vision and skills, built bridges for mutual support, and assumed a greater sense of responsibility and accountability. We have done new communication and media work and a dozen of us from diverse tribes and locales — Alaska, Navajoland, South Dakota, Oklahoma, Minnesota and Canada — are working on a new Sunday school curriculum for Native American youth. We have created models for ecumenical ministry and we are sharing old, honored traditional values on the relatedness of all creation.

Almost 20 years ago Vine Deloria Jr. called for more involvement of Indian people in Indian ministry decision-making. Much has come to pass; much must yet be done. Another General Convention held in Detroit — in 1961 — created a forum which called for the church to respond to the deepening social and spiritual needs of Indian people, and for development of leadership committed to work for creative solutions to those needs. There is still great need:

American Indians have the highest rate of suicide among any ethnic group.

Indian children die in the early months of their lives 3.5 times as often as the national average.

Reauthorization of the Indian Health Care Improvement Act (first enacted in 1975 to elevate Indian health care to a level equal to the rest of the U. S.) has been stalled in Congress for five years.

Death rates for Indians under age 25 are almost four times higher than among non-Indians of the same age.

Alcohol and substance abuse among American Indians is highest among any ethnic group.

Unemployment on 291 reservations in 1987 stood at 60 percent.

Off-reservation unemployment stood at 26 per cent.

New furtive forms of racism attack treaty rights.

The Browning era mission imperatives, calling for new programs for evangelism, justice, communication, stewardship, interfaith dialogue, education, and partnership, clearly apply to the spiritual crisis of Indian Country.

Perhaps the greatest need is for evangelism. If 92 per cent of today's Native Americans are unchurched, as the 1985 *Missions USA* report claims, we together — Indian and non-Indian — are challenged to approach evangelism with a new resolve to honor the commitment of the Episcopal Church's English forebears to bring the gospel to the peoples indigenous to America.

I. Chronology of Anglican/Episcopal mission to Native Americans in the United States

1579   Gospel first preached by clergy of Church of England to an assembly of American Indians by chaplain to Sir Francis Drake on coast of northern California.

1587   Manteo, first American Indian convert to Church of England, was baptized at Roanoke, the lost colony.

1606   James I issued charter for Jamestown colony, first permanent English settlement; ordinance deemed a purpose of colony to preach and plant true word of God among savages according to rites and doctrines of Church of England.

1613   Pocahontas baptized on Maundy Thursday while being held hostage in Jamestown harbor.

1622   English abandoned missionizing, entered extermination policy in Virginia following Indian uprising.

1644   John Eliot began Indian work in Massachusetts; continued until his death in 1695; translated Bible into Algonquin language; established 14 "Praying Towns."

1696   Trinity Church in New York City organized; one of its early rectors translated Book of Common Prayer into Mohawk language.

1704   Society for Propagation of the Gospel in Foreign Parts sent its first missionary, Thoroughgood Moore, to Iroquois nations of New York state.

1712   First chapel for Mohawks erected at Fort Hunter; Queen Anne sent altar silver. Church of England mission spread to all six of Iroquois nations.

1743   The Rev. Henry Barclay reported that only a few Mohawk remained unbaptized.

1746   Sir William Johnson named the crown's Indian commissioner in New York and exercised tremendous influence on his Mohawk brother-in-law, Joseph Brant, who remained loyal to church and crown during revolutionary War, moving to Ontario following war, and responsible for founding St. Paul's of the Mohawks, first protestant chapel of province. Brant translated English prayer book into Mohawk language.

1816   John Henry Hobart, Bishop of New York, founded first American Indian mission of Episcopal Church among Oneida, then in New York. Hobart later ordained Eleazar Williams who was likely Mohawk but claimed to be the lost Dauphin of France.

1823   Oneidas exiled to Wisconsin; Episcopal Church went with them. Hobart Church was first consecrated building of Territory of Wisconsin.

1834   First Episcopal services held in present Diocese of Idaho at Fort Hall, agency offices for Shoshone-Bannock Reservation.

1852   Enmegahbowh with Dr. James Lloyd Breck established St. Columba's at Gull Lake, Minnesota. This mission to the Ojibwa became the mother mission west of the Mississippi in Indian work.

1857   First Anglican mission in today's Alaska established at Metlakatla in Canada, moved in 1887 to U.S. territory.

1859   Bishop Jackson Kemper ordained Enmegahbowh to diaconate. Henry Benjamin Whipple consecrated first bishop of Minnesota; served in that capacity for 42 years; known as "Apostle to the Indians."

1860   First mission among Santee Sioux founded at Redwood, Minnesota.

1862   U.S. government failed to forward treaty-obligated rations and annuities to Santee; conflict followed. First Indian prison ministry when Bishop Whipple confirmed 100 Santee in Fort Snelling prison.

        Anglican missionaries arrived at Fort Yukon; when Episcopal missionaries arrived in 1896 they found groundwork laid with translations of Bible and prayer book.

1863   Episcopal Church accompanied exiled Santee to Dakota Territory.

1867   In Minnesota, Enmegahbowh ordained as first American Indian priest of the Episcopal Church.

1868   First full-blooded Santee Sioux, Paul Mazakute, ordained to diaconate; next year to priesthood. Good Shepherd on the Onondaga Reservation in New York organized.

1869   Rising Sun, an Ojibwa, began his long quest for an Episcopal missionary on Turtle Mountain Chippewa Reservation in today's North Dakota.

1870   First Niobrara Convocation held at Church of our Most Merciful Savior on the Santee Reservation; by 1872 Episcopal mission among Sioux extended to Yankton, Crow Creek, Cheyenne River and Lower Brule Reservations, along with work at Flandreau and mission among the Ponca.

1871   U.S. government ended treaty-making era after negotiating some 650 treaties with some 350 Indian nations.

        After a decade of high visibility in Indian advocacy, Bishop Whipple whipped the Episcopal Church into action; participant in the controversial Grant Peace Policy which apportioned tribes to church denominations for education and "acculturation." Between 1871 and 1882, the Episcopal Church sent 80 missionaries to Indian country and ordained 20 Indians to the diaconate and two to the priesthood.

1872	William Hobart Hare consecrated bishop of Niobrara, nongeographic jurisdiction over the Great Sioux Nation. When he died in 1909, there were 100 Indian congregations where there had been nine; 26 Indian clergy where there had been three.
1874	George Armstrong Custer led 1,200 cavalrymen into Black Hills in violation to terms of 1868 Treaty of Fort Laramie. Expedition confirmed presence of gold.
1875	Mission extended to Rosebud Reservation in South Dakota.
1876	June 25: Battle of Little Big Horn, Sioux Victory Day.
1877	U.S. government illegally confiscated Black Hills; in 1980, U.S. Supreme Court ruled the taking of the Black Hills unconstitutional.
1877	Mission extended to Pine Ridge Reservation.
1881	David Pendleton Oakerhater, Cheyenne, ordained to diaconate in New York; returned to Indian Territory and for 12 years was the only Episcopal presence in the land which became Oklahoma. Served 50 years as deacon among Cheyenne-Arapaho.
1882	Work begun at Sisseton-Wahpeton Reservation in South Dakota.
1883	Mission started at Wind River Reservation with arrival of John Roberts, a Welshman, who would remain at the Wyoming reservation for 60 years.
	Episcopal mission extended to the last of the South Dakota reservations with work begun on the Standing Rock.
1884	Sherman Coolidge graduated from Seabury and became first Arapaho ordained; returned to Wind River to work among his own people and establish St. Michael's at Ethete, Wyoming.
1885	Rising Sun's long quest realized for mission to Turtle Mountain Chippewa.
1885	First Oneida, Cornelius Hill, ordained to diaconate; 1903 ordained to priesthood.
1887	Dakota students returned from Eastern study and initiated mission on North Dakota side of Standing Rock Reservation, leading to founding of St. Luke's at Fort Yates and St. James' at Cannon Ball.
	Mother mission of Episcopal Church in Alaska established at Anvik; first United Thank Offering helped to build Christ Church in 1889.
1889	Episcopal Church assumed work begun interdenominationally among Shoshone-Bannocks at Fort Hall, Idaho; established Church of the Good Shepherd.
1890	Second Alaska mission founded: Point Hope on the Arctic among the Eskimo. It was not until 1964 that the first Eskimo was ordained to priesthood — Milton Swan.
	Wounded Knee Creek, South Dakota (December 29): Around 350 hungry and disarmed Indians slain and buried in common grave.

Seventh Cavalry sustained 25 fatalities. Action motivated, in part, to suppress further spread of Ghost Dance religion based on teachings of a Paiute medicine man called Wovoka.

1891   Fort Totten mission established in North Dakota. In Alaska, mission brought to Tanana, 800 miles up the Yukon.

1896   Work began in Nevada among Pyramid Lake Paiutes; almost all of the tribe converted to Christianity.

1897   Hospital opened at Fort Defiance, Arizona; first Episcopal mission among the Navajo. Funded originally by Westchester N.Y., branch of Women's Auxiliary.

Work began in Utah on the Uintah Reservation; in early years of 20th century 90 per cent of Utes were confirmed Episcopalians.

1899   Standing Rock Sioux Episcopalians journey to Fort Berthold to evangelize Arikara leading to founding of St. Paul's mission.

1901   Good Shepherd on the New York Seneca Cattaraugus Reservation established.

1907   Mission to Monacans of Bear Mountain, Virginia, organized by a priest's son who aspired to be a missionary to Japan.

1917   Second Navajo hospital opened at San Juan Mission, New Mexico.

1923   Initial Navajo work in Utah started; reactivated in 1942 with arrival of Fr. Liebler at Bluff.

1929   Work began among Eastern Creek near Atmore, Alabama.

1930-1958   More mission work ceased than began.

In the "relocation" area, distant dioceses such as California and Chicago organized urban outreach. One of the few worshiping communities was at Good Samaritan in San Francisco which was served by a Native American priest, Robin Merrill. When he departed, the congregation slowly dissolved.

1958   General Convention ordered a special study of the church's Indian work policy.

1961   General Convention passed nine resolutions on Indian work.

1965   National Advisory Committee on Indian Work appointed; produced *The American Indian in the Mission and Ministry of the Episcopal Church*.

1968   *More Real Involvement* document issued; established framework for future Indian mission.

1969   National Committee on Indian Work established; the Rev. George Smith (Ojibwa), chairman; Kent FitzGerald, executive director.

1970   Coalition 14 formed to receive block grants from national church through dioceses; became major funding source for Indian mission.

1977   First sustaining diocesan Committee on Indian Work organized in Oklahoma; during the decade 10 other provincial, diocesan or congregational committees were formed.

1984   Oklahoma I Consultation, jointly sponsored by NCIW and Coalition 14 in Oklahoma City.

       In addition to work earlier established in Minnesota, the mid-1980s saw new urban Indian mission organized in Denver, Portland, Albuquerque.

1985   Eighteen Bishops and Indian leaders issue Evanston Covenant, a new model in Native American seminary study at Seabury-Western Theological Seminary; seven enrolled autumn 1986.

1986   Covenant of Oklahoma II issued at the second joint consultation in Oklahoma City when 85 church leaders, including 50 Native Americans, set guidelines for Native American mission and ministry for the future.

1987   New networks formed including Mountains and Desert Regional Ministry, Urban Indian Caucus and Clergy Coalition.

       Province VIII Indian Commission revitalized; Province VII Indian Commission authorized.

II. Indian treaty rights

by William C. Wantland (Seminole)

bishop of Eau Claire

One of the greatest problems facing Native Americans is the problem of treaty rights. The average non-Indian citizen of the United States assumes that, somehow, treaty rights involve special consideration for Indians, or the granting of special rights not granted to other citizens.

The United States Commission on Civil Rights, in its June, 1981, report, made the following observations in regard to the backlash against Indians in the 1970s:

> *Many reasons have been given to explain and to justify the backlash. One explanation argues that, although there is a significant reservoir of sympathy for their situation, excessive political and material demands by Indians have soured the basically favorable disposition of the American people. From this viewpoint, it is said that the backlash is not racial or even political but is, rather, opposition to the excesses of the activists. An "equal rights" theory is often advanced to argue that Indian political power and control over Indian destiny is antithetical to the American system of equality and that Indian interests must give way to those of the larger society.*
>
> *Many individuals in the Indian world have placed a different construction on the backlash. They argue that the non-Indian interests, both governmental and private, that have been unfairly profiting at Indian expense have found their individual advantages disrupted by Indian legal and political victories and have organized to recapture their preferential position. In this view, the backlash is identified as a vocal minority of vested interests.*

A major difficulty in evaluating what has appeared to be a backlash against Indians is that most Americans do not have any frame of reference for distinguishing normality from change. Mel Tonasket, of the Confederated Tribes of the Colville Reservation in Washington, has stated:

> *I think a lot of the backlash coming from the common citizens is mainly out of ignorance because of the lack of educational systems to teach anything about Indians, about treaties. . .When the population really doesn't know what the rights are and what the laws say, they have to make judgment decisions based on what the media puts out to them or what a politician says.*

143

Chairman Arthur Flemming of the U.S. Commission on Civil Rights observed after listening to several days of testimony on Indian issues from a range of citizens in Washington state:

It is clear to me from the testimony we've listened to, that there are a great many adults who do not have any understanding of the treaties, of tribal government, and the implications of it, and so on, and they are reacting from a position of no knowledge.

This lack of knowledge and ignorance of treaty rights was also reflected by the American Indian Policy Review Commission of the U.S. Senate in 1977:

One of the greatest obstacles faced by the Indian today in his drive for self-determination and a place in this Nation is the American public's ignorance of the historical relationship of the United States with Indian tribes and the lack of general awareness of the status of the American Indian in our society today.

Alvin Ziontz, a member of the Indian Rights Committee of the ACLU, makes it clear that the arguments against Indian treaty rights predicated on the idea that such rights deny rights to other Americans are without any logical legal standing:

As a matter of principle, there is no conflict whatever between Indian treaty rights and the 14th Amendment, none whatever. The 14th Amendment says simply that if you're going to have different treatment of different groups, there must be a rational basis for that difference. There is obviously a rational basis for the separate treatment of Indian groups, and that basis is the transactions which they made with this nation. They have in effect entered into a contract, and it is no more a denial of my 14th Amendment rights that Indians continue to receive the benefits of the agreement they made than it is a denial of my rights that any group that sold land to the United States Government get paid for their land.

What, then, is the basis of Indian treaty rights? And how does that basis affect the relationship between Indian peoples and other Americans?

At the time Columbus "discovered" the New World, the North American continent was inhabited by over 400 Indian nations and tribes. These Native nations were sovereign in every respect, and were treated as such by most of the European nations. Treaties were entered into by the European and Indian governments.

A treaty is a contract between sovereign nations, and assumes a certain level of equality between the contracting parties.

After the independence of the American states and the establishment of the present U.S. government, the United States continued to make treaties with Indian nations as agreements between equals. Indeed, the Indian population was as great as the white population at that time. It is generally recognized that treaties as between equal sovereigns were made by the United States with Indian nations until the time of Andrew Jackson.

Thereafter, treaties were made by the United States as a dominant sovereign, and the Indian nations were seen as dependent sovereigns. The United States Supreme Court, in fact, declared Indian nations to be dependent or quasi-sovereign governments in its landmark decision of *Worcester v. Georgia* in 1832. Thereafter, until 1871, treaties were made with Indians primarily to obtain cession of land, or to limit Indian rights. Even though many of the Indian nations were never at war with the United States, and therefore were never defeated in battle, the treaties made during this period were never made as between equals. Not one treaty gave any advantage to a single Indian government. By the time Congress canceled the treaty-making process in 1871, well over 600 treaties had been made between the United States and the various Indian nations.

Perhaps it would be wise to review the legal effect of treaties and the place of Indian treaties in 20th century American law.

Article II, section 2, clause 2 of the U.S. Constitution declares:

> *The President shall...have power, by and with the advice and consent of the Senate, to make treaties, provided two-thirds of the Senators present concur...*

Article VI, section 2 of the Constitution provides:

> *This Constitution, and the laws of the United States which shall be made in pursuance thereof; and all treaties made, or which shall be made, under the authority of the United States shall be the Supreme Law of the Land.*

Treaties, as the "supreme law of the land," are therefore superior to the law of any state. As the Constitution says, in regard to treaties:

> *The judges in every State shall be bound thereby, any thing in the Constitution or Laws of any State to the contrary notwithstanding.*

While the United States continued to make treaties with Indian nations until 1871, there had long been complaints from the U.S. House of Representatives that agreements with Indians should involve the representatives as well as the senators. Largely due to these complaints, in 1871 Congress passed what is now *25 USCA 71:*

> *No Indian nation or tribe within the territory of the United States shall be acknowledged or recognized as an independent nation, tribe, or power with whom the United States may contract by treaty; but no obligation of any treaty lawfully made and ratified with any such Indian nation or tribe prior to March 3, 1871, shall be hereby invalidated or impaired.*

This statute ended the treaty making period of Indian-U.S. relations. However, the statute kept all previous treaties in full force and effect. For a number of years after the 1871 act, the United States government entered into "agreements" with various Indian nations. These agreements were virtually the same thing as treaties, except ratification was by both House and Senate of the U.S. Congress, as well as by the legislative body of the Indian nation. For example, in December of 1897, an agreement was executed between the United States and the Seminole nation of Oklahoma providing for allotment of a land in severalty. This agreement was ratified by the General Council of the Seminole nation and by the U.S. Congress in the summer of 1898, and has the same effect as a treaty.

However, after 1903, with very few exceptions, the United States ceased making agreements, and simply passed legislation through Congress which imposed upon the Indian nations whatever terms or conditions the government wished. The basis for this action was the provision of Article I, section 8, clause 3 of the Constitution: "The Congress shall have power. . .to regulate commerce with. . .the Indian tribes. . ." In 1903, the U.S. Supreme Court, in the case of *Lone Wolf v. Hitchcock,* declared that the commerce clause of the Constitution gave to Congress "plenary power" over Indian nations. The result of this decision was that Congress may unilaterally repeal treaties, remove Indian people from their land, or even take the land. As recently as 1953, Congress has unilaterally taken rights away from Indian nations and partially abrogated solemn treaties by granting certain Indian sovereign rights to the states without the knowledge or consent of the Indian nations [PL-280].

In spite of the "plenary power" clause of the Constitution, however, and the fact that virtually every Indian treaty has been limited or broken, the Indian treaties still remain a part of the supreme law of the land, and are generally upheld in the courts of the United States. Indeed, these treaty rights mark the whole basis for the existence of Indian nations, and the rights and privileges of their citizens.

Unfortunately, most non-Indians assume that Indian treaties made a grant of special rights or privileges to Indians, and therefore are unfair. The truth of the matter was set out by the Supreme Court in 1905: An Indian treaty is "not a grant of rights of the Indians, but a grant or rights from them" *[U.S. v. Winans].* The purpose of an Indian treaty was not to give rights to the Indians but to remove rights they already had.

Nearly every treaty made involves the cession of land by the Indian nation to the United States. In the cession of land, the Indian nations agreed to give up the land in exchange for the protection of rights not specifically surrendered in the treaty, and in exchange for payment. The payment made by the United States might include money, but often also included payment of health or educational services. Thus, the provision of health and educational benefits to Indian nations is not a form of welfare, but a sort of paid-up insurance policy — a policy paid for by the Indians with millions of acres of land.

Two recent examples might illustrate the concept of reservation of rights. In the 19th century, Indians in Wisconsin and Washington state entered into a series of treaties, ceding land to the the United States, land which the Indians owned totally and completely. Such ownership is called "fee simple absolute" ownership in legal terms. When a landowner has fee simple absolute title, the owner may sell the full title to a buyer, or may sell only a partial interest in the land, reserving the rest of the title to himself. We are all familiar with the land owner who sells the surface interest in land, but retains (or reserves) the title to the minerals under the land. While the surface owner has the right to farm and to build on the land, the former owner, and his heirs forever, have the reserved right to go on the land and prospect for the minerals.

The Washington and Wisconsin treaties reserved to the Indian peoples and their descendants the right to hunt and fish on the ceded land, just as the mineral owner had reserved the right to drill for oil or mine for coal. When the state governments and the non-Indian citizens challenged these reserved rights in the 1960s and 1970s, the U.S. District Courts [the *Boldt* case in Washington and the *Voigt* decision in Wisconsin] affirmed the treaty rights of the Indian nations. These affirmations have been upheld by the Circuit Courts of Appeals.

In spite of the fact that the treaties are clearly the law of the land, and the federal courts have upheld these treaties, and the treaty reservations follow simple real property law principles, numerous local governments and citizens' groups have attacked these treaty rights. These attacks have resulted in numerous acts of physical violence and racist actions against Indian peoples. The backlash of the 1970s has carried over to the 80s. Tragically, these racist actions reflect total ignorance of treaty rights, as noted by the U.S. Commission on Civil Rights in its 1981 report.

The Episcopal Church has been very aware of these matters, and at the General Convention meeting in Anaheim, California, in September of 1985, Resolution B-007a was passed as the stated policy of the church. Because of its importance, that resolution is reproduced in full:

Whereas, *The United States of America has entered into solemn treaties with many Indian Nations and Tribes, which treaties have*

147

been duly ratified by the U.S. Senate, and become the supreme law of the land; and

Whereas, *in these treaties, the Native American people have reserved unto themselves and their descendants certain rights, including hunting and fishing rights, water rights and health and education benefits, in exchange for the cession of most of their land; and*

Whereas, *continuously since the days of Chief Justice Marshall, Indian Nations within this Republic have been recognized as "dependent sovereign nations," entitled to internal autonomy; and*

Whereas, *Native American people currently face a growing tide of racism, erosion of treaty rights, and constant attacks on tribal sovereignty and self determination; and*

Whereas, *Native American members of the Episcopal Church are asking the Church to speak out; therefore be it*

Resolved, *the House of Bishops concurring, That the National Committee on Indian Work be instructed by the 68th General Convention of the Episcopal Church to request all agencies of the Church to advocate and support the honoring of all Indian treaty rights and the right to internal autonomy and self-determination of Indian Nations and Tribes.*

Thus, the Episcopal Church recognizes the treaty rights of Indian nations and peoples, and advocates and supports the honoring of those rights. The church must work to educate its own members, and all citizens of the United States, to understand and respect these treaty rights. As the 1984 Oklahoma Consultation on Indian Ministries observed:

> *The average person is ignorant of Indian Rights, and is ignorant of his ignorance.*

It is this "ignorance of ignorance" which we, as Christians, must combat.

III. Native American spirituality

by the Rev. Steve Charleston (Choctaw)

In 1836, an Episcopal priest was sent out by the Foreign and Domestic Missionary Society to report on progress at the church's Indian mission in Green Bay, Wisconsin. His trip was difficult. The mission itself was on the edge of what was then considered the American frontier. After weeks of travel, he arrived at the Episcopal school and met with the local clergy and teachers. He talked with the Indian students and visited their tribal community. Encouraged by what he saw, his report was positive, including one important piece of advice. He informed the members of the society that Christian contact among American Indian people could never really succeed until the church's representatives fully understood the Indian culture. They must be able ". . .to go into the heart of the Indian country; acquire their language, conform to their habits, and thus gain their confidence." In other words, they must be good cross-cultural ministers.

The Rev. Mr. Dorr was ahead of his time. Looking back from our own historical vantage point, his position seems perfectly sensible. But a hundred and forty-five years ago it was a radical notion. This was the great era of the missionary. The Christian movement in America saw itself as an agent of civilization; its duty was to convert the American Indian, not necessarily to understand him. The idea that white clergy should "conform" to the native culture was highly suspect. After all, missionaries were there to teach the Indians, not to learn from them. They were bringing the benefits of European religion and civilization into the wilderness. They were bringing the truth. What was there to learn?

The answer, of course, is that there was a great deal to learn. The tragedy of the American missionary movement, and indeed, the tragedy of most historic Indian-white relations, is that so many lessons were ignored. The exchange of cultural information, the sharing of insights and perceptions, was rarely achieved. Instead, the two cultures were pitted against one another. The hope that centuries of independent cultural development might be brought together was extinguished by one of the most protracted and bitter conflicts in human history. The space between cultures became a no-man's land of cultural genocide.

But why did this have to happen? Why was cross-cultural understanding so difficult to accomplish in America, even on the religious front?

Historians, both Indian and white, have advanced many explanations. They have traced the origins of America's cultural warfare back to the nature of European colonialism, to religious strife since the time of the Reformation, to political rivalry between the superpowers of the 17th century. Greed, intolerance, and racism are noted by-products of the cross-cultural disaster. Gold, land, furs, trade routes, waterways and railways, strong points on the map: they have all been identified as contributing factors to the Indian-white conflict. But whichever thread we choose to follow, they all weave into the same fabric. The loss on both sides was immense. The American Indian civilization was forced into a collision course with the European culture and the wreckage of that encounter still litters the moral landscape of this nation.

Vine Deloria Jr., one of the most articulate contemporary Indian thinkers, has said that, "Before any final solution to American history can occur, a reconciliation must be effected between the spiritual owner of the land — the American Indian — and the political owner of the land — the American white man." The key word is *reconciliation*. The inescapable fact of Indian-white relations is that the two cultures are radically different. They cannot be seen as identical and any attempt to force a resolution between them is bound to break down into cultural strife. Political domination of the land by white America has not resulted in the cultural assimilation of Indian America. At best, Indian people have only retreated into cultural strongholds. From there they maintain their moral claim to cultural integrity over against the values of the larger society. Indian people, therefore, are not victims of American history, but the survivors of that history. They have endured every assault against their traditional way of life; American Indian culture has survived the loss of a land base, political autonomy, religious freedom, economic patterns, and in some cases, even of language. It has adapted, but it has not abdicated. Consequently, the two historic cultures of this continent still exist in relatively the same positions they occupied almost 500 years ago. They are deadlocked. Only through reconciliation can this status quo be broken. The central issue confronting us, therefore, is not cultural supremacy or legitimacy but cultural reconciliation.

The question, of course, is how is this to be achieved? How can a reconciliation be effected between two apparently mutually exclusive cultures?

Before suggesting an answer, I believe it is important to understand the real magnitude of the problem. The American Indian culture and the European culture are polar opposites. By any test of cultural standards, they stand 180 degrees apart. This fact has been analyzed in depth by social scholars of both cultures; an itemized comparison of the cultural variations has kept anthropologists, ethnologists, and social scientists in business for years. The scope of their work is far beyond what we need here. For the sake of brevity, we can condense the bulk of the evidence into much more simplified form. Specifically, we can abstract the comparative differences between the two cultures into symbolic frame of reference. These cultural symbols reflect major aspects of both cultures and serve to illustrate something of the substantial difference between them.

The first set of symbols can be the *vertical* as opposed to the *horizontal*. we are speaking here of the sociology of culture, the way that a group of people organize themselves into a community, the way that they look at themselves from the inside out.

In a rough scheme of things, the society imported to America from Europe was vertical. That is, it was organized along the hierarchical structure traditional to European nations at the time of the first colonization of this hemisphere. The building blocks of the culture were stacked one on top of another according to social standing: the landless poor, the artisans, the landed gentry, the aristocracy, and the royal families. This was the culture of classes that many Europeans sought to escape by coming to America, but they brought it with them as part of their cultural baggage. It was implicitly maintained in their understanding of what defined a community. Even in the popular religious mind of that age, the order of things was decidedly vertical: the natural world, animal life, mankind, the angels, and ultimately, the Trinity. Life was conceived in stair steps, and a person could move up or down economically, politically, socially, or even spiritually.

On the other hand, the largest number of Indian societies in North America were horizontal. Either as agricultural or hunting societies, the Indian people of this continent organized themselves along communal lines. It is not surprising that even as late as the 19th century when Frederich Engles was seeking models for the perfect "communized" society, he chose an American Indian culture as one prime example. Rarely in traditional Indian culture was social standing dictated by birth. Economically, the direct needs of the community dictated the division of labor. Family responsibilities, through the network of clans, tended to radiate out along lines of the much documented extended family characteristic of Indian culture.

Symbolically then, the two cultures were organized along very different patterns. It would be dangerous to make too much out of the visual aides of "vertical" and "horizontal," but they do point to the inherent dichotomy between Indian and white society. Part of the problem of Indian-white relations is reconciling these two divergent social structures. Moreover, this is not just an historical dilemma. White Americans still refer to "getting ahead" or to "moving up the social or professional ladder;" American Indians still operate from the broad base of the extended family with all of its attendant restrictions and obligations. What this means is that generations of cultural evolution, although parallel after 1492, have not erased the fundamental distinctions between the two cultures. Both cultures continue to maintain significantly different definitions of themselves. Simple contact and the passing of time has not provided for cultural reconciliation.

There is one area where the two cultures reach their nearest proximity: the religious dimension. In the spiritual context of culture, the Indian and white societies narrow the gap which appears so mutually exclusive on other fronts. We can illustrate this point symbolically: If the cross can be seen as a symbol for western European religion, then the circle can represent the Indian tradition.

The cross was carried by early European colonists, both Roman Catholic and protestant, into the Indian world. As a cultural-religious symbol, it was rich with spiritual connotations; it embodied the concepts of salvation, redemption, and brotherhood so central to the European Christian faith. But even more importantly for cross-cultural concerns, it was an *inclusive* symbol. It was universal. Christ died on the cross for all men; or, as Paul expressed it, in union with Christ Jesus ". . .there is no such thing as Jew and Greek, slave and freeman, male and female; for you are all one in Christ Jesus." The sign of the cross, therefore, cast a long shadow across Indian country, but it held out the promise that ownership of its religious message was as available to Indian people as it was to the European immigrants. It is exactly at this juncture that real hope for cultural reconciliation existed, for the Indian religious view was also inclusive. It was equally universal. The symbol of the circle, as a metaphor for the basic unity of life, the drawing together of all people and things as creatures of God, was common to North American Indian culture. It too carried a message of "good news" for Indian people: that we are all one. The pervasiveness of the circle as a sign of faith was as standard among Indian societies as the cross was to European peoples. Indian encampments were arranged in a circular pattern; the kiva of the southwest was circular; tribal council grounds were circular; the sacred "four directions" formed a great cosmic circle, just as the seasons encircled human life in the natural world. The circle was a definitive religious statement for Indian culture in symbolic form. As such, it echoed the same proclamation of unity to be heard in the Christian understanding of the cross. The two symbols were compatible variations on the same theme, and they offered the most concrete chance for cultural contact available to early Indian-white relations.

Unfortunately, cultural symbols are only as good as the people who use them. The theoretical compatibility of the cross and circle was not realized in practice. As we have seen, the weight of cultural differences was thrown against the fragile links between Indian and white society. The mind-set of most early Christian missionaries precluded an acceptance of Indian religious symbolism or insight. White missionaries were products of their own cultural milieu, and despite the inclusive nature of the Christian message, they tended to offer the cross to Indian people as an either-or proposition.

Today, we have come a long way from the time when Dorr made his journey to a small Indian mission in Wisconsin. And yet, the same problems of mutual understanding and respect still haunt us. After centuries of contact, the split between the two cultures remains unhealed. The arena of cultural struggle may have shifted from the battlefield to the courtroom but the tension is just as severe. In fact, rather than having made progress toward cultural reconciliation, we are rapidly moving in the opposite direction. The divisions are growing wider and more pronounced. A dangerous retreat to the trenches of the 18th and 19th centuries is occurring that may well see a resumption of cultural cold war in this decade. Conflicts over Indian land, hunting, fishing, and treaty rights have greatly accelerated. As this nation becomes increasingly desperate for new sources of energy, it turns toward significant deposits of coal, oil, uranium, and natural gas to be found on Indian land. Indian people have become far more aggressive in asserting their legal and moral rights; the result has been an increase in violence on the borders between Indian communities and white communities. Racism is endemic. A white backlash against Indian people grows just as Indian people prepare for another round of cultural warfare. In short, the contemporary situation is approaching its critical mass. Something has to give. Unless we can achieve cultural reconciliation, and in a short amount of time, it seems likely that America will experience a social explosion between the races.

Of course, in saying this, we have come back to where we began. How can this be accomplished? How can we defuse the tension between the cultures before they erupt?

The first step must involve a return to the religious forum which has always been our closest point of contact. This is the place where the two cultures can begin the delicate process of cultural negotiation. The spiritual frontier which separates Indian and white America is by far the less volatile. People of good faith and conscience can still cross the cultural boundaries here and meet one another on an equal basis. As Dorr said some one hundred forty-five years ago, this is where we can learn to trust one another. And without trust, there is little hope that any other channels of communication will succeed. We are speaking of cross-cultural *ministry*. Ministry from both sides. Reconciliation is the business of ministry. The task of forging links between cultures falls to those men and women, both Indians and white, who take ministry as a serious vocation for their lives. They are the potential go-betweens who can cross over cultural lines. They are the representatives who can translate cultural differences into a language that is intelligible to both sides. And more importantly, they are the messengers who can return to their respective communities to carry on the work of reconciliation from the inside out. Having the confidence of their peers, they can begin to defuse tensions, combat racism, and strive for social justice in the best tradition of their religious heritage.

Cross-cultural ministry in this style is a far cry from the either-or mentality of the last century. It presents the Christian person with a difficult challenge to be both teacher and student at the same time. The dogmatic paternalism of white cultural superiority has to give way to a realization that no one group of people enjoys a monopoly on religious truth. In turn, the innate "suspicion factor" among Indian people which dictates that if it is white it must be wrong has to be replaced by an openness to accept new ideas and concepts without prejudice. In each case, historical lessons must be learned if they are not to be repeated. The bitterness and hostility of the past is a fact of life. It won't simply go away. But that does not mean religious discussion is frozen in time. Neither culture exists in a state of suspended animation. Ministry can be reshaped to meet present reality; it can transcend the past.

Already, the groundwork for cross-cultural ministry has been laid within the Indian community. As late as 1974, there were only two American Indian students attending major Christian seminaries; today, there are ten times that number in training for the ordained ministry. Religious dialogues between traditional and Christian Indian leaders have increased dramatically. A consortium of Christian Indian people from many denominations, known as the Native American Theological Association, has begun producing curriculums and theological statements that reflect the native perspective on the whole range of Christian thought. Indian clergy and laity have assumed decision making positions on the national level for many churches. Liturgies are carried out in traditional languages; ecumenical gatherings among Indian people cross not only denominational lines, but tribal lines as well; North American Indian involvement in religious issues has become international as more Indian people enter into discussion with theologians from Central and South America. The "Indian church" is no longer the stepchild of western Christianity, dependent and unsophisticated, but a full grown partner in the joint mission of cross-cultural ministry.

As we look ahead, we know that we are entering an age when cross-cultural ministry will become a necessity for all Christian churches. America has changed its mind. It has turned from its image of the melting pot and adopted a cultural view that more closely resembles a patchwork quilt. Ethnic and racial diversity is celebrated; people are increasingly conscious of their unique cultural differences; they have gone off in search of their roots. The American Christian movement reflects this new attitude. It no longer goes out to other societies, offering them a take-it-or-leave-it gospel, but invites ethnic cultures in, welcoming their special contributions to the whole Body of Christ. The future growth of Christianity on this continent depends on the success of this new approach in ministry. The rapid proliferation of cultural identities already strains the orthodox definitions of the American church; a much more flexible, and consequently a much more pluralistic structure will have to be developed. Issues confronting Indian-white relations, therefore, are not isolated or backwater concerns for American Christianity. They are symptomatic of the fundamental dilemma facing all denominations. How well we reconcile this original culture conflict may well influence how successful we are at healing our other wounds.

IV. A survey of Native American Episcopal ministry: 1987

ALASKA —   Twenty-seven predominantly American Indian/Alaska Native congregations; active Alaska Native Advocacy Committee; 100th anniversary of mission in summer 1987.

ARIZONA —   Prospects for organization of new urban ministry in 1988.

CALIFORNIA —   Worship community meeting regularly at St. John the Evangelist in San Francisco.

CENTRAL GULF COAST —   St. Anna's, near Atmore, Alabama, has served Eastern Creek congregation since early 20th century. Diocese has made VIM commitment toward Native American seminary education.

CENTRAL NEW YORK —   Church of the Good Shepherd on the Onondaga Reservation, founded in 1868; a communicant represents eastern U.S. on NCIW.

CHICAGO —   St. Augustine's Indian Center has long provided major social outreach; provides "community" for Indian seminarians at Seabury-Western.

COLORADO —   Urban congregation, Living Waters, through major cooperation of Lutherans in 1987 installed Native American priest.

EASTERN OREGON —   In association with Diocese of Oregon Indian ministry; border community human relations project planned.

EAU CLAIRE —   Leadership to Wisconsin Tri-Diocesan Indian Committee; high visibility in Treaty Rights Advocacy.

FOND DU LAC —   Holy Apostles on the Oneida Reservation is largest and oldest Indian congregation in U.S. with 2,150 baptized; part of Wisconsin Tri-Diocesan Indian Committee.

IDAHO —   Century old Church of the Good Shepherd mission on Shoshone-Bannock Reservation at Fort Hall; part of Mountains and Desert coalition.

IOWA —   Indian congregation at St. Paul's in Sioux City, a Jubilee Center. Operates health and social outreach programs.

LOS ANGELES —	New beginning with ecumenical focus; resident Ojibwa priest active in reorganization.
MILWAUKEE —	Involvement with Wisconsin Tri-Diocesan Committee on Indian Work. Bishop visible in advocacy on Ojibwa treaty rights. Indian families active in All Saints' Cathedral and St. John's in Milwaukee.
MINNESOTA —	Strong and vital diocesan Committee on Indian Work; 16 Ojibwa and Dakota congregations including two urban congregations in Twin Cities; trailblazing ecumenical models.
MONTANA —	New American Indian outreach launched; linkage with new Mountains and Desert coalition.
NAVAJOLAND AREA MISSION —	New energy in leadership development and youth programs; 1988 General Convention proposal drafted and approved by ECN Council calls for increased autonomy.
NEBRASKA —	New Jubilee Center in Gordon, Nebraska; All Saints' on Winnebago Reservation houses halfway house.
NEVADA —	St. Mary's on Pyramid Lake Reservation serves century-old Paiute congregation; resident priest.
NORTH DAKOTA —	Five predominantly Indian congregations on four reservations; joint diocesan urban programs. Active North Dakota Committee on Indian Work.
OKLAHOMA —	Strong, vital Oklahoma Committee on Indian Work since 1977. Whirlwind Mission of the Holy Family, founded by Oakerhater has ministered 100 years to the Cheyenne-Arapaho.
OREGON —	Stabilized new interdenominational Portland congregation with regular worship services; strong linkages with Ecumenical Ministries of Oregon.
RIO GRANDE —	New urban congregation founded 1985; full-time missioner funded by diocese. Strong leadership from congregation to national church networks.
SAN DIEGO —	New energy emerging with focus on ecumenical projects; diocese formerly aided interdenominational social outreach.
SOUTH DAKOTA —	Historical center of Native ministry; 89 reservation congregations; potential for new urban programs. Niobrara deanery has two NCIW representatives.

SOUTHWESTERN VIRGINIA —	St. Paul's near Amherst has Monacan congregation dating back into early 20th century. Church Army resident priest.
UTAH —	Mission on Uintah Reservation uninterrupted at Holy Spirit, Randlett; reactivated in 1987 after almost a decade at St. Elizabeth's, Whiterocks.
WESTERN NEW YORK —	Church of the Good Shepherd on the Seneca Cattaraugus active since 1901. Networking reactivated in 1986 with only other Indian congregation in state of New York.
WYOMING —	Two congregations on Wind River Reservation: St. Michael's among the Arapaho and St. David's among the Shoshone.

Provincial and regional Indian work

PROVINCE VIII	A revitalized Commission on Indian Work, primarily targeting development of new urban ministry. Holds regular annual meetings in conjunction with provincial synod.
PROVINCE VI —	Provided strong leadership for decentralization of Native American work of the national church through encouraging establishment of field office.
PROVINCE VII —	Indian Commission recently established.
MOUNTAINS AND DESERT COALITION —	Designed as coalition for mutual support in dioceses of Idaho, Montana, Nevada, Utah and Wyoming, each with but one or two Indian congregations.

V. Reflections of the first American Indian bishop

by Harold Stephen Jones (Santee Sioux)
bishop suffragan, Diocese of South Dakota (retired)

The thought never occurred to me in college and seminary days and moreover as deacon and priest that I would ever be asked to submit my name for nomination as bishop in the Episcopal Church. On September 25, 1971, at a special diocesan convention meeting in Trinity Church, Pierre, I was elected suffragan bishop of the Diocese of South Dakota, and on January 11, 1972, I was ordained and consecrated to this great office in St. Joseph Roman Catholic Cathedral, Sioux Falls, on one of the coldest nights of the new year.

After serving for four years, I was forced to retire because of a stroke while on one of many trips. The thought of having to retire early in my episcopate was very difficult to comprehend. Occasionally, I have been asked to reflect on my active years as bishop as well as the years following. I find this very difficult! After much prayer and thought I have to say that I was called by Almighty God through his people, the church in South Dakota. As to why I was called, only Almighty God knows! Perhaps Hodding Carter (1907-1972), speaking on the role of our parents, gives a partial answer: "There are only two lasting bequests we can hope to give our children — one is *roots* and the other is *wings.*

With my one-day-old brother, Kenneth, we were orphaned at the sudden death of our mother and the remarriage of our father a few months later. Our new home was with our grandparents, the Rev. and Mrs. William Holmes, missionaries on the Santee Sioux Indian Reservation. Grandfather arrived with his three aunts and the steamboat filled with countrymen from Minnesota following the so-called "Minnesota Massacre" of 1862. The group had been imprisoned by our federal government as participants. Through the combined efforts of Bishop Henry Whipple and Congregational missionaries and with permission from President Abraham Lincoln, these prisoners were permitted to come up the Missouri River by steamboat in 1866. The Rev. Samuel D. Hinman and the Riggses and Williamses chaperoned the group and established schools to train native leadership. Bishop William Hobart Hare, missionary bishop of the Episcopal Church, arrived in 1873, and found an established mission. Later, the bishop traveled westward, to the Yankton Sioux Indian Reservation and established a second church school, St. Paul's, to match St. Mary's of Santee. In these two schools grandfather Holmes received his education.

Grandmother Rebecca Hobbs Holmes was born in Decatur, Nebraska. Her father, Lorenzo Hobbs, left his ship-building trade in Boston, Massachusetts, to become an early pioneer of the state of Nebraska, where he continued his trade and found time to become one of the Nebraska legislators. At the death of great-grandmother Hobbs, my grandmother came to Santee, Nebraska, to live with her sister, who had married the first doctor on the Santee Reservation. Grandmother found work at the Santee federal boarding school.

On January 10, 1884, grandfather and grandmother were united in marriage by Father Fowler. Theirs was one of the first intermarriages in Dakota Territory. They left shortly thereafter for the Rosebud Sioux Indian Reservation, where grandfather taught at the first Indian day school, at Okreek. There my mother, their first child, christened Ida Edna, was born. Around two years later, my grandparents moved to the Moreau River area day school on the Cheyenne River Sioux Indian Reservation. While serving there, he met the Rev. Edward E. Ashley who eventually served our Dakota people for 57 years. Grandfather Holmes was inspired by this great man to study for the ministry. He served as lay reader for many years, which led to his ordination to the diaconate and priesthood. He served as special assistant to Dr. Ashley, especially, in the area of translating, especially in the preparation of the Niobrara Course, a five-year course of study and lessons to be used throughout the Niobrara Deanery. Too, grandfather served on several committees of the district and deanery.

Grandmother Holmes was a great help to grandfather as wife, mother and help in organization of work, guilds, church school and work with our youth. She became a very fluent speaker in the Dakota language. She was one of the originators of the plan to create school for Indian boys from which some might choose the ministry. This was finally accomplished in 1928 when Bishop Hare Mission Home was established in Mission, South Dakota, on the Rosebud Sioux Indian Reservation, and her two grandsons were amongst the first students.

Living with my grandparents was a unique and rewarding experience! The Holy Trinity was the foundation of our home. Holy Baptism brought everyone into God's family. Each person is endowed with God-given talents which being dedicated to Almighty God can be used by him for the spread of his kingdom on earth.The family theme seemed to be, "Seek ye first the kingdom of God and all things will be added unto you." Secondly, the education of the mind was paramount under and with the direction and assistance of God, the Holy Spirit. Truly, my grandparents offered the "Two lasting bequests" that Hodding Carter spoke of — **roots** and **wings!** Moreover, our grandparents were living examples of all that is good and worthwhile in human life!

It was my privilege to have been able to work at St. Mary's School for Indian Girls, Springfield, South Dakota, for my room and board while beginning my college career. It was an honor to know some of our finest Dakota girls. One beautiful girl, raised in the Badlands of our state, was Blossom Thelma Steele. After graduating from St. Mary's she attended Southern State Teacher's College, where at the beginning of her second year she was chosen homecoming queen. Eventually she became my wife and help-mate in my ministry.

Opportunity to serve was given me in serving 18 years in Niobrara Deanery, the Pine Ridge and Cheyenne River missions of the church as deacon, assistant priest and superintending presbyter. I served twelve and one-half years as vicar of Trinity Church, Wahpeton, North Dakota, and as director of Christian education at the federal Wahpeton Indian Boarding School, located in an off-reservation area, where around 400 students from 14 different reservations were educated. My task was to work with the non-Roman Catholic students and faculty in the school. I represented the Christian Children's Fund: approximately one-half of the student body were members of this program. I gained the support of the non-Roman Catholic churches in the city of Wahpeton. Our Episcopal students usually totaled around 100 each school year. Part of my job was to integrate them into our church school program, our youth program and our worship services. This was challenging and rewarding.

In 1968, I was asked by the Home Department of the national Church Center, New York, the bishop of Arizona and the *ad hoc* committee of Good Shepherd Mission to the Navajo, to come there as their vicar. My wife and I visited the mission and decided to leave North Dakota to try a new area. This was a real challenge to us, and we enjoyed this for over three years.

I shall be eternally grateful to Almighty God, the Episcopal Church in general, and the Diocese of South Dakota for wanting us to return to our home state of South Dakota and, further, after my retirement, for making it possible to live in our diocese, in Rapid City, to live and worship with our people.

VI. The National Advisory Committee on Indian Work, 1965-67

Officers: Kent Fitzgerald (chairman), U.S. Indian Service, Navajo Agency, Ariz.; the Ven. Vine V. Deloria (vice chair), archdeacon, Missionary District of South Dakota; the Rt. Rev. Philip F. McNairy (vice chair) suffragan bishop, Minnesota; the Rev. Clifford L. Samuelson (secretary), Episcopal Church Center, New York.

Members: Dr. Henry F. Allen, physician; Boston, Mass.; Vernon Ashley, Commission on Indian Affairs, Pierre, S.D.; John Artichoker Jr., U.S. Indian Service, Papago Reservation, Ariz.; the Hon. Robert L. Bennett, commissioner of Indian Affairs; Washington, D.C.; Ella Deloria, anthropologist, linguist and author, Vermillion, S.D.; Martin Holm, U.S. Indian Service, Aberdeen Area Office, S.D.; Mrs. Robert Horne, teacher and counselor, Naytahwaush, Minn.; William Johnston, University of Washington, Seattle, Wash.; Alvin Josephy Jr., editor, author, historian, New York, N.Y.; Robert Keller, Olympic College, Bremerton, Wash.; Francis McKinley, Arizona State University, Tempe, Ariz.; Gerald One Feather, Community Action Program, Pine Ridge, S.D.; the Hon. Ben Reifel, U.S. Congress, South Dakota; Dr. Thomas Sasaki, professor of anthropology, Johns Hopkins, Baltimore, Md.; Richard Schifter, attorney, Washington, D.C.; Dr. Katherine Spencer, anthropologist, Boston University, Mass.; Mrs. Veda Stone, Wisconsin State Health and Welfare, Eau Claire, Wis.

VII. National Committee on Indian Work

Executive Committee: Chairperson, Dr. Helen Peterson* (Oglala Sioux), Portland Urban Indian Ministry; vice chair, Bessie Titus (Athabascan), Alaska Native Advisory Committee; secretary, Dr. C.B. Clark (Creek), Province VIII Indian Commission; at-large, John Danforth* (Oneida), Holy Apostles Oneida Congregation.

Members: the Rev. Philip Allen (Oglala Sioux), Minnesota Committee on Indian Work; Ginnie Doctor (Onondaga), eastern U.S. representative; Lorraine Edmo (Shoshone-Bannock), Albuquerque Urban Indian Congregation; Tolly Estes (Dakota), Niobrara Deanery, Diocese of South Dakota; Carmine Goodhouse (Standing Rock Sioux), North Dakota Committee on Indian Work; Thomas Jackson (Navajo), Navajoland Area Mission; Cecelia Kitto-Wilch, M.D., (Santee Sioux), Niobrara ECW president; the Rev. Quinton Kolb (Ute), Mountains and Desert Region; Tim Tall Chief (Osage), Oklahoma Committee on Indian Work; Blanche Zembower (Dakota), Denver Living Waters Congregation.

1988 Incoming Members: the Rev. Mark MacDonald; Portland Indian Ministry; Jesse Torres (Oneida), Wisconsin Tri-diocesan Indian Committee.

Staff: Owanah Anderson (Choctaw), staff officer for Native American Ministries, Episcopal Church Center, 815 Second Avenue, New York, N.Y. 10017, (212) 876-8400, and Dr. Carol Hampton (Caddo), field officer for Native American Ministries, 1224 North Shartel, Oklahoma City, OK 73103, (405) 235-0728.

(* term expires, 1987)

VIII. The Covenant of Oklahoma II

We wish to characterize the spirit of our second meeting in Oklahoma City — the one we now call "Oklahoma II" — as one of hard, yet joyous work, in the context of renewal, expectation, and celebration.

For the first part of our meeting, our Presiding Bishop was with us, not only as a leader in the traditional sense, but equally as a *listener.* This, we are learning, is where all sensitivity and the collaboration from which its springs must begin. All parts of the Church must know, feel, and respond to pain in other parts of the Church.

The Presiding Bishop spoke of himself as being a bridge; and he calls us to be a bridge also. The bridge that we are challenged to be is one that, on one side compels us to articulate our needs, and recommendations for responding to those needs; and, on the other side, allows us to bring our unique gifts to the rest of the Church, and indeed, through her, to the world.

We find that relationships built upon mistrust, even when there has been ample historical justification for it, always foreordain separation; but, as trust grows, so also does hope, and with that hope, the opening of vast potential for reconciliation, healing, and wholeness.

We wish no longer to express our needs in negatively constructed terms, but rather in a positive context. Building upon this, we would like to tell the larger Church what we need, share some thoughts as to how these needs might best be met; and, in addition, even now say what we feel we have to offer the Church.

We fully recognize that *racism* is still a hideous reality in our midst, and we know there will always be elements and remnants of this among us. But, we know also that when we acknowledge and face this ominous reality, and continue to engage it, the process of redressing the damage it causes will be grace-filled and powerful. We commend our Primate for the steps he is contemplating in the inclusion of our voice in addressing the issues of racism in the leadership of our Church on the national level. We expect our Church, not excluding the diocesan level, to keep the reality of racism before it, and continually work toward vanquishing it. We acknowledge prejudicial tensions within and among our communities, and we pledge ourselves to recognizing and going beyond these.

We recognize that the Church has an existing *structure.* This is a reality, and is not undesirable, *per se.* However, we feel these structures must be challenged vigilantly in order that they become and remain open and participatory. We therefore expect our Church, on the national and diocesan levels and in local communities, to look at all structures, including the administrative and financial, related to the work in, of, any by Indian and native peoples, and make certain that these are accessible and widely participatory, especially on the part of those affected by such ministries.

We recognize that the Church needs *leadership.* We, as Indian and native peoples, need a leadership emerging from, affirmed and supported by, and responsive to our communities. Leadership development needs to be enhanced in both lay and clerical areas. We therefore expect our Church to help us design clear, well-grounded curricula and processes, endorsed and backed by recognized authority, for the nurturing of leaders in, for, and within, our Indian and native communities.

We recognize that our common baptism into Christ obligates us to a ministry of evangelism and *education,* for the joy of the Gospel-way-of-life is spread by the handing down, sharing, and redefining of knowledge, in both informal and formal ways. Our educational needs are great, with respect to both children and adults. We therefore expect our Church to help us develop educational materials and ministries geared to our particular needs.

We recognize that we have an obligation to minister to and serve one another within our own communities, and we rededicate ourselves to this in a new way. We feel that our traditions already have a wonderful stream of generosity and sharing flowing through them. We hope that this tradition can be a deeper part of our own Christian commitment. Further, we have seen the tragedy called "burn-out" in many of our finest and best leaders. We resolve to do our best to eradicate this plague from our midst, and bring forward models for well-being.

Much in our consultation has revolved around our particular Indian and native *spirituality.* We claim this spirituality as being deep and abiding. We seek the means more profoundly to proclaim this spirituality. And, we offer it to the whole Church for her renewal and refreshment. We no longer will ask for our voice to be heard — this echoes paternalism. Rather, we will raise our common voice in full confidence that the Holy Spirit, the wind, the breath of God, will carry it forward.

We cannot, however, speak of spirituality in a vacuum. Spirituality thrives upon wholeness. The larger Church has resources of a kind that will aid and assist us, particularly as these relate to the devastating multitude of social problems we are facing regarding family life, health, substance abuse (such as alcoholism), and injustice. Above all, the most treasured and treasurable resource we have within our Church is its peoples, of all ages, including children, with all languages, cultures, and diversities. For this reason, we have celebrated with joy the presence of a native Hawaiian at our consultation. We recognize that our Church is not the only communion facing enormous social problems. We will work, in every way, on an ecumenicalbasis, in the direction of the resolution of these vital concerns.

Noting that a great part of the Church's witness is *not* to permit the avoidance of painful issues, we submit the following as actions needing to be taken. We count on the whole Church to participate in bringing them into reality.

1. The continued including and empowering of Indians and native peoples in the decision-making apparatus of the Church.

2. Exploration and experimentation with, in the very near future, alternative modes of Church governance and structure.

3. Consultation in all programs of the national Church designed to combat the evils of racism.

4. Assistance in the development of a variety of media especially designed to foster cross-cultural appreciation and understanding.

5. Assistance in the design of materials and programs for the training of indigenous Church leaders, both lay and ordained.

6. Assistance in the design of educational curricula for adults and children, addressing both Church and broadly social needs.

7. The exposure of the whole Church to native spirituality, and the encouraging of native communities to offer this spirituality to the whole Church.

It was Jesus' prayer that we all be one. We finish on a note similar to that upon which we began — the word our Presiding Bishop left with us. He said he hoped he would hold up the unity of the Church as the primary vehicle of the Church's accomplishment of its mission.

We pray that native and non-native peoples alike may be called into the fullness and unity of Christ, and the grace of reconciliation, through the offering and sharing of their respective God-given gifts with one another.

Given at Oklahoma City
October 10, 1986
by the participants of
Oklahoma II
in unanimous consent

The Rt. Rev. Craig B. Anderson
Howard Anderson
The Rt. Rev. Robert Anderson
Uberta Arthur
Mary Ellen Baker
The Rev. Joe Bad Moccasin
George Baldwin
The Rev. Henry Bird
Norman Blue Coat
The Ven. Noah Brokenleg
The Rev. Gary Cavender
Paul Chalk
The Rev. Steve Charleston
Blue Clark
Lydia Conito
John L. Danforth
Virginia Doctor
The Rev. James H. Dolan
The Rev. Thomas Doyle
James Eckels
Lorraine Edmo
The Very Rev. Clyde Estes
Gaye Leia Ezzell
The Rev. Andy Fairfield
The Rev. Virgil Foote
Duane Fox, Sr.
The Rt. Rev. Wesley Frensdorff
The Rev. Canon Patrick Genereux
The Rev. Hal Greenwood
The Ven. Robert Herlocker
The Rt. Rev. Harold Hopkins, Jr.
The Rev. Barney Jackson
Thomas Jackson
Rosella Jim
The Rt. Rev. C.I. Jones
Gladys Kassionas
Gard Kealoha

The Rt. Rev. Rustin Kimsey
Gordon Kitto
Lloyd LeBeau
Monte Littlefield
The Rev. Gerald Mason
The Rt. Rev. Gerald N. McAllister
Mary Ellen Meredith
Alonzo Moss, Sr.
The Rev. Edward F. Ostertag
Donald Peter
Helen Peterson
Duane Pinkerton
Elsie Pitka
The Rev. Steven Plummer
The Rev. Ruth Potter
Christine Prairie
Mark Raymond
The Rev. Canon Victor Richer
Marie Rogers
Buford Rolin
Dean Mark Sisk
Tim Tall Chief
Michael Taylor
Marilyn Teiken
Bessie Titus
The Rt. Rev. Richard Trelease
Mary Jo Turgeon
The Rev. Gary Turner
Lillian Vallely
Erma Vizenor
The Rt. Rev. William Wantland
The Rt. Rev. James D. Warner
The Rt. Rev. Roger White
Kathleen Williams
The Rt. Rev. Steward Zabriskie
Blanche Zembower

Church Center Staff
The Most Rev. Edmond L. Browning, Presiding Bishop
Owanah Anderson, Staff Officer, Native American Ministry
The Rev. Richard Chang, Administrative Deputy to the Presiding Bishop

The Rev. Richard Gary, C-14 Liaison
Carol Hampton, Field Officer, Native American Ministry
Barry Menuez, Senior Executive for Missions Operations
The Rev. Earl Neil, Executive for National Mission in Church and Society
Whitney Smith, Video and Audiovisuals Producer

Oklahoma II Consultation — October 6-10, 1986

Jointly sponsored by the National Committee on Indian Work and Coalition-14

IX. *Bishop Whipple's letter to President Lincoln*

1862

TO HIS EXCELLENCY THE PRESIDENT OF THE UNITED STATES.

Sir: We respectfully call your attention to the recent Indian outbreak, which has devastated one of the fairest portions of our country, as demanding the careful investigation of the Government.

The history of our relations with the Indian tribes of North America shows that after they enter into treaty stipulations with the United States a rapid deterioration always takes place. They become degraded, are liable to savage outbreaks, and are often incited to war.

It is believed that much of this record has been the result of fundamental errors of policy that thwart the Government's kind intentions toward this helpless race. We therefore respectfully call your attention to the following suggestions: —

First, That it is impolitic for our Government to treat a heathen community living within our borders as an independent nation, instead of regarding them as our wards. As far as we know the English Government has never had an Indian war in Canada, while we have seldom passed a year without one.

Second, That it is dangerous to ourselves and to them to leave these Indian tribes without a Government, not subject to our laws, and where every corrupt influence of the border must inevitably foster a spirit of revenge leading to murder and war.

Third, That the solemn responsibility of the care of a heathen race requires that the agents and servants of the Government who have them in charge shall be men of eminent fitness, and in no case should such offices be regarded as a reward for political services.

Fourth, That every feeling of honor and justice demands that the Indian funds, which we hold for them as a trust, shall be carefully expended under some well-devised system which will encourage their efforts toward civilization.

Fifth, That the present system of Indian trade is mischievous and demoralizing, and ought to be so amended as to protect the Indian and prevent the possibility of the sale of the patrimony of the tribe to satisfy individual debts.

Sixth, That it is believed that the history of our dealings with the Indians has been marked by gross acts of injustice and robbery, such as could not be prevented under the present system of management, and that these wrongs have often proved the prolific cause of war and bloodshed. It is due to the helpless red men that these evils shall be redressed, and without this we cannot hope for the blessing of Almighty God in our efforts to secure permanent peace and tranquility on our Western border.

We feel that these results cannot be obtained without much careful thought, and we therefore request you to take such steps as may be necessary to appoint a Commission of men of high character, who have no political ends to subserve, to whom may be referred this whole question, in order that they may devise a more perfect system for the administration of Indian affairs, which shall repair these wrongs, preserve the honor of the Government, and call down upon us the blessings of God.

(Signed by Whipple, 18 other bishops and 20 priests and lay persons)